The Lucky Ones

THE LUCKY ONES

African Refugees' Stories of Extraordinary Courage

Anne Mahon

GREAT PLAINS
PUBLICATIONS

Great Plains Publications gratefully acknowledges the financial support provided for its publishing program by the Government of Canada through the Canada Book Fund; the Canada Council for the Arts; the Province of Manitoba through the Book Publishing Tax Credit and the Book Publisher Marketing Assistance Program; and the Manitoba Arts Council.

Design & Typography by Relish New Brand Experience
Printed in Canada by Friesens
Photography by Keith Levit

Library and Archives Canada Cataloguing in Publication

Mahon, Anne, 1965-

        The lucky ones : African refugees' stories of extraordinary courage / Anne Mahon.

Includes bibliographical references and index.
ISBN 978-1-926531-72-4

        1. Africans--Manitoba--Biography. 2. Refugees--Manitoba--Biography. 3. Courage--Case studies. I. Great Plains Publications II. Title.

FC3400.A24M34 2013   305.9'06914097127   C2012-908065-9

MIX
Paper from
responsible sources
FSC® C016245

ENVIRONMENTAL BENEFITS STATEMENT

Great Plains Publications saved the following resources by printing the pages of this book on chlorine free paper made with 10% post-consumer waste.

TREES	WATER	SOLID WASTE	GREENHOUSE GASES
1	312	20	58
FULLY GROWN	GALLONS	POUNDS	POUNDS

Environmental impact estimates were made using the Environmental Paper Network Paper Calculator 3.2. For more information visit www.papercalculator.org.

You gain strength, courage and confidence by every experience in which you
really stop and look fear in the face. You are able to say to yourself,
"I have lived through this horror. I can take the next thing that comes along."
You must do the thing you think you cannot do.

— ELEANOR ROOSEVELT

It is what we make out of what we have, not what
we are given, that separates one person from another.

— NELSON MANDELA

The author is donating all proceeds from the sale of this book back to the African community of Winnipeg through two local charities: micro-lending opportunities for business and community projects at SEED Winnipeg and entrance bursaries through the University of Winnipeg's Opportunity Fund. Visit annemahon.ca for more information.

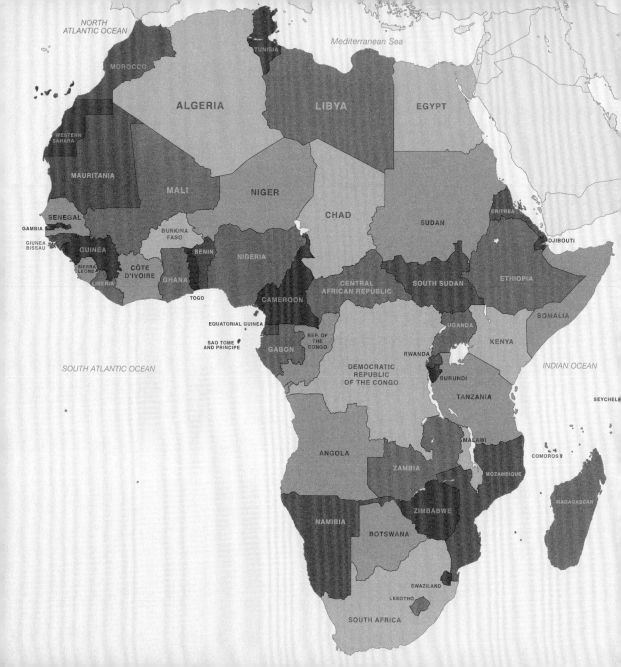

Table of Contents

Foreword

Last year Canada welcomed 248,000 newcomers to our shores of whom 27,000 came as refugees. Of that number, Manitoba received 16,000 new immigrants, over a thousand designated as refugees.

These are significant numbers for our country and for the province that Anne Mahon and I live in. They represent an infusion of talent, resources and eager new citizens to fill out our big spaces.

If you combine this newcomer demographic with the fast-growing First Nations/Métis/Inuit population, you can readily see that the old paradigm of Canada as a bilingual, bicultural country no longer applies. We are experiencing a transformation of monumental and exciting proportions.

Canada has historically taken a broad approach to immigration and refugee policy, supported over the years by governments of different policies and persuasions. Next to Medicare it may be one of our defining traits as a country.

I recall the advice of Ron Atkey when I took over the portfolio of Employment and Immigration from him in 1980. He said I was being handed "a sacred trust" that required great care in order to keep a consensus among Canadians on the vital importance of immigration.

Today, Canada remains the country of choice for many people around the world and the number of new arrivals remains impressive; yet it would be fair to say that while there is broad acknowledgement of the benefits to Canada from the newcomers, we don't know much about them – where they are from, what experiences they bring, what customs, values and beliefs they espouse. For refugees especially, who arrive from war-torn lands, many have been persecuted, have lost family members, have little in common with the country they now call home. Arriving in Canada is both a blessing and a shock. And for most Canadians, used to living in the privilege and comfort of Canada, there is often little awareness or understanding of the life of a refugee and the challenge of making an adaption to a new place.

The Lucky Ones: African Refugees' Stories of Extraordinary Courage is a welcome contribution to bridging that divide. As a volunteer, Anne Mahon began to listen to the stories of African refugees that have come to Manitoba over the past several years as part of the province's accelerated policy of immigration. She has gathered the stories of a cross-section of individuals, expressed in their own words, and fashioned a fascinating portrait gallery of exceptional people who have come here to start anew.

This is a book that tells of courage, persistence and hard work as these individuals escape the toils and tribulations of conflict, family breakup, hunger and deprivation in the refugee camps, and the daunting task of starting a new life. We learn of the tragedy of losing close family in a hail of bullets from drug-riddled militia in Somalia, the repressive government of Ethiopia's efforts to intimidate dissident journalists, the chaos of living in the murderous region of eastern Congo. And in each case, the necessity to seek safety by pulling up stakes and beginning an odyssey that would often take years before a secure place could be found. Each story is different, each has a gripping reality to it, each of the individuals comes through as an ordinary man or woman, faced with extraordinary circumstances and showing unusual powers of strength and perseverance.

Through each of these stories we also learn of the admirable and often unsung work done by a constellation of individuals and institutions to help the refugees escape from risk and find a new home. The incredible work of the United Nations High Commissioner for Refugees, for example, which acts as the key organization in ensuring there are refugee sanctuaries. The many civil societies, church groups, aid agencies that provide food, clothing and protection remind us how much we owe to a worldwide network of helping hands that give agency to the care and wellbeing of refugees.

What is also an encouraging and essential dimension of the refugee story is the enormous effort made by each of the storytellers to establish roots in Canada, work at several jobs to make ends meet, form local community associations to help newer refugees as they arrive. And above all, it is the determination to pursue education for themselves and their children that dominates each tale of how resettlement takes place.

There is no doubt how important the desire for education is and how crucial assistance from the governments, aid agencies, schools and universities is in making that education accessible and culturally relevant. For example at my own university, our faculty of education offers special programs for teaching children from war-torn societies.

The book doesn't present the stories as all sweetness and light. There are many expressions of frustration and struggle in finding proper housing, learning the language, obtaining accreditation for academic qualifications. Feelings of a lingering guilt find their way into the stories about family and friends left behind. And there is a refrain of regret at not being given opportunity to meet Canadians, other than a caseworker, teacher or volunteer. These are people who want to be respected and involved as Canadians, and all too often feel isolated.

But these little platoons of worry and concern are greatly outweighed by the statements of thankfulness at being in Canada, along with a strong determination to make meaningful contributions both to the ever growing refugee community and to Canada in general.

One of the individual stories in the book is about a young Somali man named Muuxi Adam. I know Muuxi, as he is an Opportunity Fund student at the university and had been deeply involved in a wide variety of student projects, including mentoring African students. Just before Christmas, he was awarded the Sybil Shack Human Rights Youth Award given by the Manitoba Human Rights Commission for his work in helping newly-arriving refugees. His goal in graduating is to help those in Somali, still struggling to survive within this failed nation. He epitomizes what is so evident in this book – the spirit and commitment these refugees bring to this country. They are making an instant contribution in our community. They bring with them a set of connections back to Africa that will help Canada to develop its global presence, and establish important relations in that continent that is going through such a transformation.

In Anne's words, she uses the title *The Lucky Ones* to describe how the people she has written about felt in being here – using the word "lucky" as in "being blessed." We too are blessed in having them here, adding their energy, their talent, and their unique understanding of Africa, just as we are fortunate to have Anne Mahon's book to introduce us to such an impressive group of Canadians.

Lloyd Axworthy
President, University of Winnipeg
former Minister of Foreign Affairs

Author's note

A number of things came together serendipitously to bring me to the writing of this book. In 1998, I moved with my family to another Canadian city after having lived my entire life in Winnipeg. During our three years there, I missed my hometown very much and struggled with the adjustments of living away from it.

This event would prove to have even more of a deep and lasting effect on me than I could have predicted. A second factor in the creation of this book occurred one day in late 2006 when an African friend told my family and me some of his life story. His history – including twenty-five years of separation from his family and country, and the courage it took to rebuild his life in Canada – had a profound effect on me and became one of the main motivators that drew me to envision this project. His story reminded me how relatively easy my relocation and transition away from home had been compared to Africans who come to Canada. I could drive, I understood English, my family had financial stability and I knew the culture for the most part. Because of this realization, I became extremely curious about what refugees from another continent could be feeling. I felt compelled by my connection to him and the painful truths he shared that day. At that time, I was searching for something to immerse myself in that felt meaningful, and an idea unfolded.

I had a vision of writing a book with a mosaic of amazing stories much like the one I had heard. I imagined my proceeds from this book being donated to micro-lending opportunities and post secondary bursaries for Africans in the Winnipeg area. So in 2007, I decided to interview Africans and record and write their personal life stories, but only after first researching how to best write the book.

I began to call people I had never met who were better acquainted with the African and refugee worlds in order to meet and question them. I did not realize it at the time, but during this research phase I was laying the groundwork for finding participants. I carefully considered how to interview, how to respect other cultures, and how to write so the reader would be captivated by these stories and the subjects would be properly honoured. But these concerns receded over time as my skills and conviction in the book grew.

All stories in this book are in the subjects' own words, carefully written as much as possible from what they said in their taped interviews. I feel privileged to be the messenger of these stories. It is a surprise – especially to me – that I am the vehicle for these shared stories since I am from outside the African community. Yet I am a volunteer, a supporter, and now a messenger. This book is a collaborative effort, similar to what Canada is at its heart … people coming together from diverse backgrounds to share and build.

Africa is a continent of many distinct countries and certainly thousands of cultures with constantly changing political and social issues. It is not the goal of this book to present commentary on these topics, which are better addressed in the daily news and on the Internet, but instead to break open the human narrative that is their result. North Americans hear mostly about Africa's problems: civil war, violence against women and children, and poverty. This book chronicles the real-life realities of some of the challenges of living in Africa. But listen carefully to the stories and another description of Africa emerges; a continent of strong cultures and traditions that value family and community first, of people working together at a grass roots level to create triumphs of humanity and of people relying strongly on faith, whether Muslim or

I feel privileged to be the messenger of these stories.

Christian. In 2011, the Nobel Peace Prize was awarded to three women, two were African: Ellen Johnson Sirleaf , president of Liberia, and Leymah Gbowee, a peace activist. They represent just some of the many people and communities working passionately to create peace and positive change.

I've learned a tremendous amount working on this book, but there are two things I am especially mindful of. We all have a great deal in common, even if we have come from very different places and cultures. The universal truths of wanting to love and be loved, to work for fair pay and to raise our families in safety apply to us all. I also learned to believe that anything is possible. The resilience of the subjects in this book, as well as this book's creation, have taught me this: we should never limit our expectations to the boundaries of what we already know.

MUUXI

Our lives make no sense if we are not helping others.

My mother, she was the backbone of our family during my childhood in Somalia. No matter how bad the situation, how difficult, she always held up her head. We were poor and the struggle was always there. When you grow up poor, you know how it feels to truly struggle. You have nothing and you expect nothing. But still you need to find a way to get something.

I grew up in the capital city of Mogadishu. Our family was made up of my mom, my five brothers and sisters and me. Our stepfather was good to us, but not around much, so my mother raised us mostly on her own. I had a special connection with her because I was her first child. My twin sister and I were the eldest. In Somali culture, the oldest son is privileged. But my mama used to tell me she did not love me because I was her oldest son, she loved me because of my heart and who I was as a person.

We happened to be part of an unfortunate generation. The government of Somalia collapsed so there was no infrastructure, no healthcare, no safety. For people in a stable, democratic society this would be very hard to understand. Our normal life was turned upside down. I remember days when we had nothing to eat, and my mama couldn't go to work – she was afraid to go out because the fighting from the war was so bad. Mama worked cleaning houses and doing laundry ten to twelve hours a day. Because of the corruption and civil war in my country there were also no public schools, only private schools, but they cost a lot of money. My mother believed in the power of education, so when she could get the money together we went to private school for short periods of time, especially in the early grades. For two years, we were somewhat lucky – the teachers wanted us there because we were "A" students and they felt for us, so they said, "Stay and bring the money when you can." It was very difficult for my mama and she tried so hard, but there were times when we just could not go to school. She would then teach us to read and write in Somali after she finished her work. She'd come home at the end of the day, and even though she was very tired, she would take a shower and give us a school lesson – how to write or how to read. We'd wait all day for her, my brothers and sisters and me. There was no daycare that's for sure, so we'd sit around, maybe play soccer and wait for my mom. If we were lucky, we might find work for a few hours. Sometimes restaurants would let us wash dishes for a meal or we would work for a bus owner. He would give us five cents for every person we could convince to take his bus to the market. Living like this was typical for a poor, young African growing up during a civil war.

The government of Somalia collapsed so there was no infrastructure, no healthcare, no safety. For people in a stable, democratic society this would be very hard to understand.

I remember one of the hardest days – it still breaks my heart every time I think about it. The war was really difficult, and there was a lot of gunfire going on so we couldn't go outside. We had gone for more than twenty-four hours without food. We had nothing, so my mom finally went out, but she came back later, still with nothing. The little kids were crying for food and milk. My little brother had found a big tomato, which had been overlooked in our backyard garden, so my mom sliced that tomato and gave it to my younger siblings. As one of the eldest, I could not take any of the tomato for myself. In my mama's face I saw that she was thinking, *I am sorry, I have nothing to offer you.* I had already seen my mom sell everything she had – her jewellery, her clothes and special things that meant so much to her. She had nothing left. It was both touching and sad for me. Watching my mother mentally and emotionally collapse was very hard, and I could not take it anymore, so I went out to find something else for us to eat. I knew that I would do whatever it took to get something for my mom that day so she wouldn't have to cry, even if it was necessary for me to steal.

I went to a market called Bakarah. Bullets flying in my neighbourhood made it very unsafe to go there, but I went anyway. I asked to carry an older man's bags of food. He said, "I don't want to give you money." I replied, "You don't understand; you have food. You give me the bags and I'll carry them for you. If you think that's helping and you can give me money, that's what I need. I am not going to beg and I do not want to steal. I am young, but I can work. Give me this chance so I can feel good about it." And he said "Wow!" He was very supportive and paid me much more

than he needed to. That night I came home with two bags full of food. But my mom, she had been worried and anxious because I had gone out into the fighting. She said she could have lost me forever. At that time, I was eight or nine years old.

At eight, my brain didn't function as an eight-year-old's, because I really didn't get a childhood. We all had to grow up quickly. I started thinking as though I was a twenty-year-old. I was tired of war. I wanted a regular life. I wanted to go to school. I wanted to know what life was like before everything was changed by the war. There is a whole generation that has grown up in Somalia and doesn't know about government, or police, or laws or rules. I wish my childhood had been like a regular child's, filled with more opportunity. A childhood where I didn't have to worry about bombs dropping on my head or seeing my family, especially the ones I loved, going through hardship. That was heartbreaking.

My mama always gave us hope things would get better. At the craziest or most difficult moment, my mom would say everything will be all right. She always said *Insha'Allah*, an Arabic word meaning "if it be God's will." My mama had a strong faith and taught it to me. She said hope is not something you can buy, but it is something you can give yourself. I would need these words of my mother's more than I realized at the time, not yet knowing what would happen in my life.

When I was fourteen, I came home one day to find neighbours screaming and crying outside my house. They told me to run away. I didn't know what to do. I didn't know what was happening. Instead I went inside and found my stepfather bleeding and dead on the floor. I felt like fainting and I had to hold myself up. My brain couldn't function. My mother and stepfather were from different tribes. I found out much later that the elders of my stepfather's tribe had wanted to take us children away, but he refused. The elders said he was no longer loyal to his clan and so later they returned and killed him.

I could not see my mom or my family anywhere. I felt dizzy, so I went outside to get away from the horrible sight of the body and when I did, two guys grabbed me, put me in a car and drove off. They kidnapped me and took me to an outdoor garage where an armed guard watched over me. I was chained to the fence – it was a very long chain so I wore it all the time. I spent the next eighteen months of my life there. I wore the same clothes on my back the entire time. If the rain came, my only protection was to sit in the toilet stall – which was really a hole in the ground with a small roof for covering. I had to fix cars and carry heavy things no kid should have to carry. I slept in the corner of the garage on a carpet. I didn't get enough food or water to drink. It was inhumane. As a hostage, I had no choice. Either I did what they asked or they would shoot me. That was my life.

The way I escaped is a miracle. Sometimes we hear about miracles and do not believe in them, but sometimes miracles do happen. There was a fight that broke out one night, close to the garage. The gunfire was so loud that the watchman ran away in fear and left me unguarded. It was at that moment that I faced the biggest decision of my life – to stay at the garage and know that I would eventually die there, or to get help. For me, believing I could get help and leave the garage, that was very difficult. But thinking about dying wasn't any easier, so I screamed for help. But it wasn't just a regular scream; it was a cry from deep within my heart. I knew it was my last chance for life. Either I would die inhumanely or I would find a way free. That night I had to be willing to sacrifice my life for the idea of freedom. When I screamed, two guys with guns finally came. I shouted "Don't shoot" and started to explain my situation, but they interrupted me, saying they didn't have time to listen, "what did I want?" I told them freedom. They shot the chain on my leg free and said "Run!" But I couldn't; after a year and a half chained to one place I didn't know how to run or where to go. They said, "What's the matter with you? Run!" My body took over and I ran. It was three in the morning, and I didn't know what to do, so I ran to the only place I knew – my family home.

When I found it, no one from my family was there, but I did find a family friend in the neighbourhood who would become the saviour of my life. He told me he didn't know anything about where my family was, but he had heard that my mother's brother who lived in Europe had been trying to locate us. This friend said that if the men who had held me hostage found me they would probably kill me. I was in danger and I would bring him danger too, so he took me to another village far away. I hid in his brother's house for over a month. I left only twice: once to speak with my uncle on the phone and a second time to buy clothes for my travels. I had never even met my uncle, but he had arranged to get me out of the country safely. I took a bus with my family friend to Mogadishu, and then on to Addis Ababa, Ethiopia. Once in Ethiopia, I was introduced to a man called an agent who would accompany me on the airplane flight. I was told to follow him, not to ask any questions and to do everything exactly as he said or he would leave me alone in this crazy world. If I wanted to meet my uncle I had to follow his orders. I was sixteen years old at the time.

Imagine my shock when I heard the flight attendant's words "Welcome to Toronto, Canada." The plane was not landing in Europe! I was not going to my uncle! To this day I have never met this uncle of mine or spoken to him. I wish I could contact him and thank him for saving my life. I do not know anything about him. Nothing. This is another miracle. The man accompanying me used a passport and got me through customs. I don't know how; no one told me anything about how they got me into Canada. Once in Toronto, we took a bus to Winnipeg. We arrived on a cold day in October. As we stood

outside the bus depot, the agent said he was going to get some coffee. He left me there in the cold and I never saw him again. While I sat waiting, a Somali man passing by on his morning walk to work saw me. On his way back at lunch I was still there, so he spoke to me in English. He asked me if I needed some help, but I did not know what he was saying. My handler had told me not to talk to anyone, so it was a very difficult choice, but I said a few words in Somali. Thankfully, he understood me. He said he had seen a number of people in the same situation and would help me. He wanted to take me to the police, but I did not want to go, because no one trusted the police back in Somalia. I was amazed that he trusted me right away.

He took me to immigration, and I told them my story. As that man said goodbye to me that evening, he gave me his phone number and said, "Call me if you need anything." That first night I stayed at Welcome Place – a common first destination for newly-arrived refugees. It is run by Manitoba Interfaith Immigration Council who offer support and resettlement services to refugees. They found a Somali man who agreed to be my legal guardian, seeing I was underage, and I went to live with him. But the Somali community is small, and I needed help to understand the Canadian culture and system, the country and laws, so I called the man who helped me the very first day. His name was Abdi. He became my mentor and a father figure to me. He showed me what was acceptable and helped me to become the man I am today.

It takes extraordinary courage to be a refugee. I had to trust other people with my life. I could only observe; I could take no action; others were making the decisions for me. I had no choice. It was very difficult. I was only sixteen years old, and my head was spinning, constantly asking, *Is this a safe place? Am I really being helped or am I here to have someone take my kidneys in an illegal surgery?* All the questions I had! What could I do? I was alone and so lonely. My survival came down to the human connection. Sometimes with other human beings, even though we do not speak the same language, we have to trust them.

In my heart, I believe that no matter how long I live in Canada, because I was once a refugee, I will be a refugee forever. Nothing can ever change that. It is a part of my history, part of my existence as a human being. When you become a refugee once, it is forever.

I had to give up some of my culture and my beliefs to learn to live here. That could be mistaken for giving in to brainwashing, but it's not. I had to develop my own personal culture, a culture that is not my Somali culture, nor my Muslim culture, not just my Canadian culture either, but a custom mix of the best parts of each of these cultures that have made up my life. This personal culture can help me adapt to a new country or a new situation. It guides me, because I've had to learn a whole new way of living. It allows me to keep parts of my old culture and adopt parts of my new one. Canada is diverse and multicultural, and I've learned to accept all people, which allows me to make connections and friendships. Being new here, I must leave my comfort zone. Surviving is not truly living. To live fully, I must integrate. That means sharing with others, making friends, seeing our differences and our diversity.

Another very difficult experience for me as a newcomer was to learn English. Learning English is like being born one more time in

> It takes extraordinary courage to be a refugee. I had to trust other people with my life.

your life. Do you know how hard it is to be reborn at sixteen? I had to take baby steps. I had a Grade 4 education when I arrived in Canada. It was hard to be alone in Canada without my family. I did have people who cared about me, people who were helping me; I even had a father figure, but it was hard to let go of my family, especially all at once. I always had dreams of them. I thought of my happy childhood memories a lot and that gave me motivation to keep trying. Many times I heard my mother's voice guiding me and encouraging me. I knew from the bottom of my heart that I had to let my family go in that I had to live without them, but I never forgot about them. I never let them go in that way.

One day, a friend called me at home. She told me her mother who lived in Ethiopia thought she knew my family. She thought they were alive. I had known this friend for a few years, but I had never talked about my family. When I speak to people I don't talk about my problems, so she did not know much about my family situation. But through Somali community connections, she and her mother had figured this out. She said she would get back to me in a couple of days. I called her the next morning and said, "You cannot say you'll get back to me in a couple of days. Do you know what this means to someone like me? I have not seen my Mom in six years; I need to know right now." So I spoke to her mother on the telephone, and she told me to call her the next day at an agreed time. When I did call her the next morning, another woman came on the phone – it was my mother! I knew it was her because of the voice. I started shaking and sweating and I had to sit down. To this day, both my mom and I don't know what we even talked about during that first conversation. When my phone card finished, I used my cell phone. I don't know how long we talked, or what we said, but I remember how it felt. I felt that I would never be alone again. I found my own world. My mama was someone I always looked up to, so finding her was magical.

Today, I am happy. I have my own family: a wife, and two children. I work with new-comer kids in the downtown area, and I am a student at the University of Winnipeg. I have been reunited with all of my family except my twin sister, who died during my family's travels to Ethiopia. She was weak and could not complete the journey. I don't know how I succeeded through the hardships: learning

English, passing the courses, and then actually applying to university, but I did. The first day I went to university was amazing. Here I was in Canada with this opportunity! For me, university is more than a building, it is the birthplace of knowledge. It is like going into a whole world of innovation. When I sit in a classroom, I feel important. I am there for a mission; I have a responsibility to learn, to do my best, for whatever is ahead of me. Sometimes I think of myself as someone whose life almost ended. This is a second chance. I cannot mess up. This is my chance to be reborn again. The first day I went to university, I did not go only for myself, I went for my mother too, knowing the circumstances in which she raised me – working long days and teaching me at night because she wanted us to have an education.

Yes, I am lucky. Lucky to be alive and lucky to be living here in Canada. Whoever lives in Canada is a lucky person. We are *all* lucky. Coming to Canada has provided me with so many opportunities I could never have had if I was anywhere else in the world.

I am able to have peace in my heart and live as an ordinary human being; to see the sun go up and then down, and I am still living in peace. Canada provides me with the opportunity to be who I am meant to be. I can work and whatever I do is for me. Canada has given me hope, given me everything a child, a man, could think of. The people of Canada have opened their hearts to me. They are the ones who gave me a hand when I was down, a hug when I was shaking, and gave me support when I didn't know where to go. I must continue the legacy of being a Canadian by supporting others. I am also lucky because I am part of two different worlds (the one I was born in, and the one I live in now) and I have the opportunity to connect those worlds to each other. Certain circumstances come with being lucky, so it comes with a price. I feel I must help others in turn. This is why I say *our lives make no sense if we are not helping others*. It is a circle. If one person eliminates one problem, that makes a difference for someone else. My goal is to help others; not specific groups – Africans, or Asians or Muslim

> Sometimes I think of myself as someone whose life almost ended. This is a second chance. I cannot mess up. This is my chance to be reborn again.

people of my faith – but all of humankind. I was raised to look at people through their hearts, not their skin colour or religion. Everyone must be treated justly. How can I be part of that community of dedicated people, working lifelong to help others? So many people need support, especially women and children. I want to give them a hand when they need it, because I know how it feels to be alone and in need.

In 2008, I travelled to Ethiopia to be reunited with my mom for the first time in six years. The first day, she took me for a walk and I saw a lot of children doing nothing all day. I started to talk with the kids. As soon as I mentioned school, their smiles stopped and they said they had been living in these slums for five, eight or ten years and had never gone to school. When I heard that I wanted to disappear, because I knew exactly how they felt. In Africa, school is an opportunity to become who you are fully meant to be. When you are not educated, you feel in your heart you are an ignorant person. God gave us each a brain, but the brain needs guidance and education is part of that.

These children deserve a chance in the world. Unfortunately they have poor parents who cannot provide it. So my dream is to give these children hope by building schools that will provide them with education and food to eat while they are there. I remember school when I was a kid; just seeing the building was exciting! School is a place where we can see the whole world. When people have education they can understand their problems and help themselves. Children need education so they can learn to make different choices; they don't have to carry guns, they don't have to die of AIDS, and they don't have to be poor their whole lives. Building the first school is the hardest, and that is what I am struggling with right now. Not building that school, leaving it alone, means leaving the little kids alone. The longer it takes the harder it is.

When I now think of my mother's word *Insha'Allah*, I feel that everything I do is God's will, and I give thanks to God when it works out. It is part of my faith. When my mom said *Insha'Allah*, it was during very difficult situations. It taught me that no matter

> School is a place where we can see the whole world. When people have education they can understand their problems and help themselves.

what situation I am facing there is a way out, and if there is a way out today, there will be a way out every day of my life. Those hardships in life become memories, and those memories become the story of my life. I need to make a connection from that life, to this life today so I can do my best. *Insha'Allah* is both faith in God and faith in self. I think God sometimes examines our ability to function in times of hardship. Do we lose our faith, or hang on? All of us, no matter what our faith – Christians, Muslims or Jews – still have hope through our faith. Faith is the bright light that saves us during our hardships. It is also necessary to have faith in the people who surround us, because God's not going to come down from the sky and give us whatever we need. If we don't have faith in humankind, then we have no faith is God.

I don't think of myself as extraordinary. I think of myself as being like every other child, but I had good parenting. It is the little things that parents do, like the stories they tell their children at bedtime each night. Parents may not see at first the impact those stories can have, but if they have patience and God gives them the time, then they will eventually see. When I think of my life, I think that no matter how hard my situation is today, if I was able to escape that garage, I can escape any problem in my life. My mother and her words of *Insha'Allah* have taught me this.

In 2005, at the age of eighteen, Muuxi wrote and directed a one-hour movie called Ray of Hope, *which was sponsored by the National Film Board. It is the story of a teenager new to Canada, trying to please family and uphold culture, yet make a new life in North American and not be lured by gangs. The final scene of the movie is a celebration lunch with friends and family in a restaurant, sending a message of optimism, even if the road is difficult. Muuxi spent August 2012 in four African countries interviewing and filming children for his latest documentary about how war affects their lives.*

Muuxi says his mother instilled in him to love others as they are and not how we want them to be. This unconditional way to love and be loved is at the core of who he is. Muuxi has created a charity called Humankind International. They are busy raising funds to build their first school in the Dadaab refugee camp in Kenya.

The war in Rwanda had broken out in 1990 and when I returned I found that everything had changed. I felt like a foreigner in my own country. In 1994, after President Juvenal Habyarimana was killed, the fighting intensified. It was difficult for me to figure out what was going on. Tutsis were being killed, but so many Hutus were dying too. That is why I left my country. Eventually over 800,000 Rwandese would die in a few short months.

My wife and I fled first to Congo, but we couldn't live there because of the lack of safety, so we moved on to Tanzania. Our first child was born there in 1996. But the Tanzanian government made a decision to repatriate all Rwandese and was forcing them to return home. We felt that returning to Rwanda was unsafe because the civil war was still raging, so we moved on to the Kakuma refugee camp in Northern Kenya.

Have you ever watched people fight over a jug of water? Our water in Kakuma flowed from a community tap. We lined up in the morning at 7:00 a.m. to fill our containers. The ration was only ten litres of water per person per day, but still the taps could run dry before everyone got water. And they did

run dry. It was frustrating waiting for water and watching fighting and violence when there was not enough. The water was precious. We had to wash our clothes with it, take a bath with it, drink it and cook with it. The shortage was really very, very difficult for all of us. Kakuma is in a semi-arid, semi-desert zone. The temperatures could be as high as 40 c, and people would be just sweating full out.

As well, so many people in the camp were suffering from malnutrition. The food we were getting from the World Food Program was not enough; it was not a balanced diet nutritionally. There was a non-government organization (NGO) providing children with supplementary feedings – milk and porridge – but it still wasn't enough. People had left their homes with nothing, travelling hundreds of miles; so many people were without proper clothing too. It was a good thing that it was hot! There was another problem – many refugees grew up in wartime and had to retreat for safety, often to the forest. They were stressed and violent and conditioned by the killing in war. So to kill a person was normal. They had never had the opportunity to learn how to read and write in school and had never lived in a peaceful situation to know "this is right and this is wrong."

Kakuma was a multinational camp of 120,000 refugees from surrounding countries: Sudan, Somalia, Ethiopia, Uganda, Congo, Burundi, Rwanda and Eritrea. Generally, people lived in harmony despite some problems of fighting and security. Each of these cultural communities had its own area in the camp, so cultures were not mixed together. This helped a lot in controlling the language and other important parts of culture such as singing. Each community had its own representatives: chairman, chairlady, secretary and a committee of elders, and together they made up the administration. These people were chosen by the members, so they were trusted people.

I was chairman of the Rwandan community for nine years. The refugee camp is where I learned my talent for leadership. I know how to interact with people and help them and also how to manage a community. As chairman, I was like a bridge between the community and the officers of the United Nations High Commissioner for Refugees (UNHCR) who oversaw the camp. I felt proud to help people, to assist them, because there was suffering – too much suffering. People didn't know the language or how to approach the organizations. They needed someone who was committed to helping them. I was not paid; it was a voluntary job.

Communities would turn to the administration whenever there was a problem. We would then come together to talk about the issues and find a solution. If we could not find a solution we would call a community meeting and ask for suggestions to solve the problem peacefully. We also had regular meetings with the many other chairmen to talk about general problems in the camp and to see how we could help our people live in harmony. It was my honour to serve the people.

At Kakuma, my home was called a "shelter." These shelters were usually three-by-four metres, with mud walls and floors and roofs of either metal or plastic sheets. They were small, very small. There was some space between each shelter so people could sleep outside when it was very hot. Getting

> At Kakuma, my home was called a "shelter." These shelters were usually three-by-four metres, with mud walls and floors and roofs of either metal or plastic sheets.

children to sleep was a real problem. People would put out their mattresses and sleep around 2:00 a.m. when it was cool. We had mosquito nets we tucked under the mattresses so scorpions and mosquitoes carrying malaria could not get inside. Cholera was a big concern too.

People came to Kakuma from all different backgrounds. Those who grew up in the forest trying to avoid the war didn't know about sanitation, so they relieved themselves anywhere. The camp had a sanitation department and they asked people to dig a hole, and then they would give them the materials to put a structure over the hole (to make an outhouse). But these people did not understand; they needed sensitization and awareness to be able to set up the structures and use them properly. It was good that we had no rain. If we had rain, I tell you the whole camp would have had cholera.

Education was a really positive thing at Kakuma. I appreciate the help of the government of Kenya because they supported the school and allowed us to follow the Kenyan curriculum for a primary school and a secondary (high) school. A secondary school is a privilege to refugees. We even had a distance university – The University of South Africa (UNISA). I started working at the refugee camp's one high school, Bortown Secondary, as a math teacher. With my background in hydrology, I had used a lot of maths and physics. I was not trained as a teacher, but I had done a lot of tutoring in my spare time, while living in Rwanda and Tanzania. I also had the life experience of being the Rwandese Community Chairman in Kakuma. I was later promoted to be the head of the mathematics department and then the principal of the school until I left for Canada in 2007. The school was run by Lutheran World Federation, an NGO. We had no library, but we had books, a lab and a kitchen. We gave the students porridge each day because they did not have enough to eat at home. We had about seventy students for every teacher. There were over 700 students – mostly boys and about 100 girls. The lack of girls in school is a problem in the refugee

We had no library, but we had books, a lab and a kitchen. We gave the students porridge each day because they did not have enough to eat at home.

camps and in Africa generally, because the girls of the family are often looked at as house women who have to take care of the children and don't need school education. Many daughters have forced or early marriages and leave by Grade 10, if they do get to go to school.

Discipline was a problem at the school. The first years were not easy. Many boys were stressed and traumatized and violent. So we called everyone together – the teachers, and the elders of the communities. We organized a teacher-parent association. We said we cannot continue like this: a school without discipline cannot be a school. So with teams of teachers we slowly started counseling students and, finally, when I left the school, it was very nice. We had only isolated cases of indiscipline.

The students were tough, and they worked hard at their national exams. The competition was very high because one or two students would be selected each year by WUSC (World University Service of Canada) to study in Canada. It was wonderful to be able to work at the school and to see some changes in the system. I felt happy and very excited to be part of all that.

I did have many problems living in Kakuma it's true. But not everything was negative. I had people who supported me: the Rwandese themselves, and my wife's two sisters who took care of my two children and even me. We shared what we had. And I had friends there too, very good friends: the Kenyan nationals and my teachers. Even the people working for UNHCR became friends; they had empathy. Despite the problems, the camp members lived in surprising harmony. And the international community tried to do their level best to support the refugees, but they did have to focus on the emergencies. The refugee camp of Kakuma was not seen as an emergency – it had been there for so many years. There are always other world emergencies. When the budget started being cut in Kakuma, officials began encouraging people to go back to their countries. But I did not see that as an option for me and my two children. So in 2007, we left Kakuma for Winnipeg.

Here I am in 2013, living in Winnipeg and happily married too! That has been a blessing in my life. One day a friend came to my house saying, "Two ladies from Rwanda have just arrived, let us go and greet them." When newcomers first arrive in Winnipeg people go to welcome them. It was really amazing – there stood Assumpta, my friend from Rwanda. I had not seen her since I was twenty. "You are still alive!" I shouted. We hugged and kissed. It was a big surprise because during the war I didn't know where she had gone. Imagine a woman alone with two young kids travelling from Rwanda to South Africa. She had no passport, no papers, nothing, and had to pass through borders, hiding herself and her children. It was not easy. She arrived in Winnipeg in June 2008.

In January 2009, Assumpta and I were married. Now I am living in a beautiful home, I have a good job after attending Red River College and my children are going to school for free. I don't have the problems of wartime. We are finding friends. This is a multinational country, and everybody needs the support of neighbours. Canada is a country with opportunities and wonders. What I like is that Canada respects human rights and you get what you are entitled to. There is no discrimination. It is really equal and fair here. Coming to Canada is not a right, it is a privilege.

I say to people *be blessed*. I have passed through so many difficulties: security and safety problems, hunger, disease, my first wife passing away – so many problems, but I have seen the hand of God. God is really alive and helping people. I have to kneel down and say thank you God. So I say *be blessed* to everyone I meet because it is the blessings I have received from God – I want those same blessings to reach the people I meet.

Recently, I watched as Azarias spoke to a group of students at the University of Manitoba. Azarias is a very joyful person, with a big smile and friendly laugh. Giving an overview of his life's happenings, he spoke of being a young man, returning to Rwanda from his studies in the Ukraine, and taking on a position of importance in the government. Naturally he had plans and expectations after years of study. He told the students "in one day it was wiped away." *Twenty years later, I could still hear the shock and disbelief in his voice.*

SEID

*I had to put aside my memories in order to integrate.
I realized living a meaningful life in the present would be
my only chance to be part of mainstream society.*

In my home country of Ethiopia, I worked as a journalist, until one day I became the news. I was working for the state-owned television station that was controlled and manipulated by the political party in power at that time.

As their employee, my main objective was supposed to be representing their interests no matter what story I was assigned to. This was tough for me. I was young, in my early twenties then. I had graduated with a university degree in literature and journalism and was bold and fresh. When you are young, of course you are idealistic. I saw the transparencies of Western politics and wanted to make that happen in my own country. In more than eighty years, Ethiopia has had only three leaders: King Haile Selassie who ruled for more than forty years until he was ousted by the military regime of Lt. Col. Mengistu Haile Mariam, who ruled for seventeen years until the EPRDF (Ethiopian People's

Revolutionary Democratic Front) rebels became the political power eighteen years ago.

It was my dream to see Western-style politics in my own country, to see Ethiopia move forward instead of being bogged down in conflict from the hatred between tribes – those that felt inferior against those that were perceived superior. These conflicts are due mainly to the divide and rule strategy of the EPRDF. In Ethiopia, there are more than seventy different ethnic groups. If tribes are encouraged to disagree and remain separate then they stay weak, which is of benefit to the ruling political party. Everyone has become a victim of this policy. I believe in transparent and fair elections; unfortunately the votes of the people were being stolen. There were no free and fair elections in Ethiopia despite the ruling party's claims that there were. Elections were rigged.

I don't know why but I found myself assigned to very controversial issues, covering stories that were in opposition to the ruling political party. For example, I was asked to write about two specific controversies and was expected to favour the government's position. One was an educational policy that required ethnic-based learning (children from each tribe being taught in their own language only), all the while senior government officials were sending their children to Europe for education in English. The other controversy was about top university economists who were openly criticizing the government's high-priced land lease policy, which the economists thought actually deterred foreign direct investors.

I found myself at a crossroads: I worked for the state in a job that was my passion, yet I was uncomfortable and could not be the spokesman for the government's devil policies. I found myself writing the articles with a leaning towards representing the views of the public. After all, my salary was paid by the taxpayers and not the government. But of course the government didn't consider it like that; their position was *We are paying you so you must respect our interests.* But I preferred my freedom of speech. Like I say, I was young and bold. I miscalculated. I thought that if I criticized the ruling political party I might lose my job – that was the maximum risk I thought I was taking. But I was wrong. They would eventually come after me.

In 1999, there was a national election in Ethiopia. The country's constitution states that there should be no government officials within twenty-five kilometres of the polling station on voting day so that everyone's vote may be freely decided. But when voters were entering the booths, the elected politicians were inside. This was intimidating and wrong, but I knew I could not write about it or I would get into trouble, but we did decide to have our TV crew film it. We told the story without words. I had a close friend who had a friend who was politically affiliated and a newspaper editor. Every morning at the paper, the staff had a meeting to evaluate the newsworthiness of the top stories. I became pretty much an agenda for discussion: *Why is this guy criticizing the government? What is he doing?* I was a young, neutral journalist trying to represent the truth, but I wasn't seen that way. The good thing was that after the election story, my friend's friend said, "Seid is in danger, make sure he watches his back or he's going to get into trouble." I quickly realized I had to prepare myself to skip, to leave the country or I was going to end up in prison. That was frustrating because I knew the government was corrupt and fabricating charges against me, and it was also embarrassing to be presented as a criminal.

I never would have imagined I'd leave my country like that. I was university-educated, and I had a girlfriend and family I cared about. But I knew I was no longer safe. I went into hiding and began my plans to skip out of the country. I did not have money to travel or to prepare illegal documents so I had to borrow some from my cousin. I had already got a fake Ethiopian passport, but I sent a friend to the capital city of Addis Ababa to buy me something called an exit visa, which would allow me to approach the Kenyan border. So you see I was becoming involved in illegal activities because of the government's actions. During that time, an archived photo of me was circulated to regional police stations with the orders to arrest me. My girlfriend's brother knew of my planned escape, but I could not tell even my girlfriend or my family. The only other person who knew my plans was my close friend Getch. He was a judge there but later moved to New York.

> I was university-educated, and I had a girlfriend and family I cared about. But I knew I was no longer safe. I went into hiding and began my plans to skip out of the country.

The day I said goodbye to him we just looked down and wept. He was the one who told my family I had left.

My girlfriend's brother lived in Gigiga, a town lying close to the Ethiopian and Kenyan border. His family was well-known there, and when I was ready, members of the local community showed me how to cross the river to get to the Kenyan border. Leaving like that was intense and frightening. But that's the way I had to do it. I have so many people in my life whose favours I cannot repay. This bothers me every day.

In Kenya, if you have *pessa* (money) you can do anything you like. So when I reached the Kenyan immigration, I presented my fake passport and documents with the necessary bribe. The officials realized my papers were fake but they gave me a Kenyan travel visa anyway, and I crossed the border just like that.

My intention was to find a way to immigrate to North America. I was afraid to stay in Kenya for long because there were so many undercover Ethiopian police there. My girlfriend's family knew people in Kenya and asked them to assist me. They owned a restaurant and offered me a place to stay until I could find a workable solution. They recommended I approach the UNHCR (United Nations High Commissioner for Refugees) for their assistance. Two years prior I had been one of two journalists invited to cover the United Nations conference in Addis Ababa so I had the UN identification from Geneva proving I was a journalist. The UNHCR verified my press pass and assured me I had a strong case for immigration, especially because I was a public figure. They suggested I stay in their refugee accommodations but I didn't want to because I was afraid others would suspect me of spying on them seeing that I was a government journalist. I didn't want to be misinterpreted so I told them I already had a place to stay. I ended up living with the friends of my girlfriend's family for a year and a half. Unfortunately the UNHCR in Kenya had became corrupt at that time as can happen with aid agencies in poverty-stricken places and it wasn't until I contacted the International Federation of Journalists (IFJ) that my case progressed. Finally, after being interviewed I was told, "Congratulations, your second home will be Canada." Leaving there is a moment in my life I see as truly lucky.

It is hard to imagine how many other refugees I left behind in Kenya. Although I never lived in a refugee camp, I've had many friends who did. My situation – living with these people I barely knew for one and a half years – was torture enough, but many refugees have to wait and wait, sometimes for up to fifteen and seventeen years, before getting out of the camps and immigrating to a free country.

Today, I am a Canadian citizen with a Canadian passport. This passport means a lot to me because I went through so many adversities to get it. I credit this passport with freedom of speech because, no matter what, I have it and the basic human rights it guarantees; that nobody can violate. Canada is one of the greatest countries in the world. It is a peaceful country, and I am really fortunate to have this passport, this citizenship. But even with my Canadian passport I do not feel safe returning to Ethiopia. In 2006, my mother died. My family was so worried I would not be able to handle that. My friend Getch finally told me about her death. I could not travel home for the funeral because I did not feel safe. I was alone here, feeling confused and depressed, and I was having a really hard time dealing with it. That was the saddest thing.

Every day, I learn something new about this country. I don't know when I'll stop learning. I think of myself as being a blend of the cultures of my two countries. It is a weird feeling to come from a strong culture with very strong traditions and then to try to live somewhere else. I don't want to lose the part of my identity that came from my life in Africa. Of course as a newcomer, I passed through a phase of culture shock. In the beginning, I felt I should have stayed quiet, and remained in Ethiopia like all the other hypocrite reporters serving the government. I knew no one in Winnipeg, and I missed my friends and family. Sometimes you miss something as simple as a moment of your old life. In Ethiopia, there is a time after lunch when people just hang out and have coffee together. I did not fully appreciate this ritual when I left my country. But I found this tiny social activity had tremendous value in my life. These things you miss, but they don't help you here, unless you want to live in the past. But by living in the past, I was unhappy and frustrated. One day I said to myself, *Is this how I want to live for the rest of my life?* I had to put aside my memories in order to integrate. I realized living a meaningful life in the present would be my only chance to be part of mainstream society. I wanted to do meaningful work but needed a skill, so I decided to go to school in Canada. I had a degree in literature and journalism from Addis Ababa University. Writing is my passion so I went to Red River College and obtained my creative communications diploma.

There was a time as a journalist when I was ambitious and wanted to change Ethiopia, and the world. But then I realized I couldn't do it, or that it would take too much time and effort, and that I needed to concentrate on what I could do *now, here.* I don't care how much of a scholar you are, there comes a time to give back and help others. There came a point for me when I wanted to give back to the community I now live in. I see so many newcomers who have tremendous challenges and need assistance. I know I am much better off than they are with no education and little English to express themselves. But I do share the values, the experiences and the sufferings of these people who are new to Canada, so I decided I wanted to work for a service provider assisting newcomers. One of my early jobs was as a computer training coordinator. When I would show newcomers how to open an attachment and then they'd see their family photos, the excitement on their faces kept me going. Today, I work at RRC as the Manitoba Immigrant Student Coordinator serving as a link between new immigrants and the wide range of educational opportunities across the country. The times when others benefit meaningfully from my help are the moments in my life that I feel most excited.

I love to help other people. And helping others has helped me to move on with my own life here.

When I first arrived in Canada, I worked briefly at a 7-Eleven convenience store. I worked for survival; I was ambitious and knew I wanted more. There are so many skilled immigrants here with strong educational backgrounds – medical doctors, engineers, accountants. I think that with short-term training, and adequate English, the Canadian government should give them a chance to prove themselves. Those trained as nurses back home deserve to work, at least, as nurses' aides here in Canada. If newcomers' previous work experience and

> There came a point for me when I wanted to give back to the community I now live in.

education counted in some way, that would lift morale. I am fortunate, I had the advantage of my early training and found meaningful employment, but so many trained newcomers are discouraged. That is not good for the newcomers and it's ultimately not good for Canada. I would love to see more diversity in employment, especially in higher skill areas like the government for example. When newcomers see other newcomers in a more senior position it gives them great encouragement.

Still generally, if you have passion and you are determined, you can do anything in Canada. There are no limits here and everyone has a say in the political process. Here I know my vote is counted. Although there have been many challenges for me, I do not regret speaking out back in my home country. One of the journalistic ethics is to speak the truth. I spoke the truth and I am proud of it.

Seid says that one of his "wildest dreams" has always been to write a novel. When he lived in Ethiopia, he was able to travel freely and he kept reams of notes on his travels and experience. He then explained, "Those collections were my assets and I had to leave them behind. Losing those notebooks is one of the biggest losses of my life." Currently, Seid is writing a movie script in his native language of Amharic. It tells an immigration story, addressing the struggles and challenges of living in a new country.

KIVI AND GUILAINE

I do not have much to give, but I want to share with you and your family.

I interviewed Kivi and Guilaine in the spring of 2010. They had been living with their children in Winnipeg for three years. It was their idea to be interviewed together.

Listening to them share their story together gave particular insight into the strength of their marriage which they must have relied on heavily during the incredible stress of fleeing their country for safety, raising their children in extreme poverty and beginning again in Canada. Kivi points out that the refugee life and strain of resettlement in a new culture are often the cause for a number of marital breakdowns.

KIVI: It was my brother Guilaume who introduced us.

GUILAINE: He has the same name as my father.

K: When I first met Guilaine, I was twenty-eight and looking for a wife. I had been engaged to another woman a few years before, but the day of the wedding, while people were waiting in the church, my fiancée ran off with another man. I was so disappointed. After that I became discouraged. I didn't know what to do, living alone. So my elder brother, Guilaume, said, "You seem as though you are disappointed with the ladies in Bunia. Maybe it would be good to go to a different city." He said there was a lady named Guilaine where he was living and that I should come and meet her. So I travelled 750 kilometres to Kisangani where he lived. I invited Guilaine over to my brother's home. When I met her, I had a strong feeling that she would be a good wife. I had been serving God in my life since I was a boy, so I had prayed before we met that I would receive a sign, a feeling of conviction in my heart that I would know if she was the one for me. When I met Guilaine I could see that she wanted real love and not just material things from the marriage, and I felt this was confirmation that she was the right person for me.

G: I was nineteen when we met. When Kivi asked me to marry him, I did not say "no," but I did not give him a clear answer. Shortly after, Kivi returned to Bunia.

From the time I was a little girl, I had prayed to God that he would give me a good husband some day. One who would know me deeply and care for me lovingly, so that I did not have to be like many of the other girls from Kisangani who became prostitutes to earn enough money to live. Every evening, all by myself, this was my prayer.

After Kivi left, I continued to pray and go to church. One day while I was praying, in my mind, I heard God's voice say, *Since you were a little girl, you've asked me for a good husband so you do not have to become a prostitute to survive. Now I send someone to you and you say "no." You don't like the one I sent you?* During this time there was another man who also wanted to marry me, but I did not like him. I was confused. After hearing God's words, I felt like my heart started to love Kivi even though he was far away. Later, I would understand that he was the answer to my prayers; I just did not realize it at the time. Two months later, Kivi returned to Kisangani for a second time. He did not inform me that he was coming, but he sent someone to tell me he had arrived and to ask to see me. I went to where he was and we talked. I told him I would marry him, but I had one condition; he must meet my parents and agree to whatever they asked. Kivi said "yes," and came with me to meet my parents.

K: The problem was that Guilaine's parents were not ready to allow her to marry me because she would have to move to Bunia with me. They worried about what it would be like for Guilaine to live far away from her family. They had so many questions. They were not happy.

G: My parents spoke with Kivi, but they did not accept him right away because they did not know where he had come from; they did not know his family. They worried that maybe he already had a wife. Also, they did not want me to go far away. My grandfather started crying and said, "You cannot leave me. If I die who will cry for me?" So again Kivi left.

K: I never felt discouraged. I was patient and persistent, because I knew that Guilaine was the answer to the need in my heart, and that we had the same feelings and ambitions. I could understand that this was hard for Guilaine's parents. I appreciated that they did not want to let her go with just anyone; they wanted to be sure that she would be happy. I could see that they were serious and loved her very much. I liked that.

G: But a few months later, my parents came to me and said that I was grown up now. They said I needed to start a new life, in my own house, with a husband. They told me I was free to marry Kivi. They said they would have a friendly talk with Kivi to settle everything.

K: When I returned, I met with Guilaine's parents and they asked me many questions: Why did I decide to come to Kisangani to look for a wife? Were there no ladies in Bunia? What was the problem? But seeing that Guilaine had agreed to marry me, they agreed.

G: Before marrying in our country, a dowry must be paid to the bride's family.

K: We have 520 tribes in the Democratic Republic of Congo (DRC), so we have 520 different cultures. Each tribe has its own ways. Many tribes ask for a dowry of cows, but the people of Guilaine's tribe were not farmers, so they asked for a dowry of money, five goats, clothes and some food. I had my own business – I was an evangelist at my church, I produced and sold recordings of myself and others preaching, and I drove a

We have 520 tribes in the Democratic Republic of Congo (DRC), so we have 520 different cultures.

taxi – so I was financially okay. Getting the dowry for Guilaine was not difficult.

Guilaine's family would not allow her to go to Bunia by herself. They wanted someone from her family to accompany her and see her future home, so they would know where she would be living.

G: We were married in 1992 in Bunia. By then, about a year had passed since we met, and we were really in love. My auntie brought me to Bunia – she represented the family. My eldest sister was living there too, so she came to the wedding as well. When I arrived in Bunia I did not go straight to Kivi's home, I went to my sister's. Then Kivi and his family came to meet me and my elder sister at her house. We had a ceremony in a church and then dinner together. Afterwards, I moved into Kivi's house to begin our life together.

Today, we have six children of our own, as well as our nephew, Blaise. Kivi's brother died many years ago, when our nephew was just five. Christian, Joe, Blaise, Rachel and David were all born in Congo. Bahati and Elijah were born later in Uganda. We have just one girl and six boys!

κ: The DRC has spent many years at war. There is both tribal war and political war. Tribal war is what led us to leave our country. I belong to the Hema tribe and those from the Lendu tribe were systematically killing my people. It became very unsafe for us. One day while we were at home, our house was attacked. We had to run. We had no time to gather anything. If you had one shoe on and one shoe off, that's how you had to run. Our two eldest children, Christian and Joe (then eight and six), were at school at the time of the attack, so we became separated. There was no time to go to the school to find them, and we could not return to our home. We just had to go. The town of Bunia was very close to the Ugandan border, so that was the natural place to cross over and escape from Congo. And it was not just us fleeing. There was a mass of people on foot, running, fighting off attacks, scared, some even dying on the way. But by the grace of God we managed to cross over.

We left Congo with nothing: no clothes, no documents, no money, not even a single coin. We quickly grabbed the younger children who were home with us at the time – Rachel, David and Blaise – and ran. We arrived in the village of Paidha in Uganda. We spent our first night there in a church. As servants of God, we thought it would be a good idea to look for shelter there first. The pastor was away at bible school, but his wife and family took us in and gave us a small place to pass the night. Over time we would become close friends with her husband, Barnard, the pastor. We were there just three days. After that, they said we had to look for somewhere else to live. It was too difficult for the wife, who was on her own, to house us long-term, so we found a place to rent. But there is very little work in Uganda, and as a refugee with no papers it was difficult to find any kind of job.

We heard news and information from the radio and from people arriving from Congo. We believed Joe and Christian were still in Congo, but we did not know where. Sometimes I felt I should return to Bunia and look for the boys, but it was impossible to go back; it was so dangerous. Guilaine said I should not return; instead we must pray.

> We left Congo with nothing: no clothes, no documents, no money, not even a single coin.

There was nothing we could do, but I felt conflict inside me.

G: It was a tough year living in Paidha. Kivi was often away looking for work or pastoring to churches far from home. We had three young children and very little food. The living conditions were terrible. The news we received from Congo and Bunia was discouraging: more and more people were being killed, especially women and children. Every day I cried, thinking to myself that Christian and Joe must already be dead. I had no one to talk to and I started having panic attacks. Finally Kivi decided to take me to the hospital. There was no hospital in Paidha, so we travelled fifteen kilometers to another village named Goli. Kivi knew my hospital stay would cost money and we did not have any, so he left me there and went off to try to find work. I stayed in the hospital two weeks. We brought David, our youngest child with us and he was admitted too. He was just one year old. He was given intravenous fluids because he was so dehydrated. He cried a lot, wanting to be held, but I did not have the strength to carry him. I cried a lot in the hospital too. I don't even know who looked after Rachel and Blaise back home. Someone must have come and taken the two children to their home. And then there were my thoughts of Joe and Christian back in Congo. That was perhaps the most difficult of all. Family are expected to assist the patient in the hospital, but I did not have any family members there, and I could not care for myself. Friends from church and neighbours came. They would help me to bathe, and carry me to the bathroom because I did not have the strength to walk by myself. People brought food and prepared everything for us. Many did not speak my language, so there was no way for us to understand each other. God just sent them to help me at that time. It is a miracle to me – here I was in another country I had never visited and was helped like that. I felt sure that the hand of God was present at that time.

> It is a miracle to me – here I was in another country I had never visited and was helped like that. I felt sure that the hand of God was present at that time.

K: When I returned to the hospital, I found my wife and son being assisted. People from my church had made contributions to pay for the hospital bills.

G: At home one night a short time later, about 10:00 o'clock, there was a knock at the door. It was dark, I had no light and I could not see anything. Kivi was away, and the children and I had gone to bed. I called out, "Who is that?" I heard the voice of our pastor friend Barnard. He said, "Open the door, I have a visitor." I thought *Aaah, what kind of visitor will come and visit me at this time of night? I do not have food or a light!* I felt annoyed. There was a very small amount of kerosene in my lamp, just enough for a minute or two of light, and I found one match in my pocket. As I was lighting the lamp in my bedroom, I heard the door open and shouts of "Mom!" I immediately knew it was Joe. In ran Joe and Christian too. We hugged each other and started to cry together. Crying and crying. I kept saying, "It's okay, it's okay."

Finally I asked how they got there. And they told me the story. Their Uncle Job (he is a friend but our children call our male friends "uncle") had found them wandering the streets of Bunia on the day we had to flee.

Job was a businessman and friend from our church there. Around the time we escaped, he was trying to get out of Congo too. On his way to the airport, he saw Christian and Joe on the road and asked them where their father was. They said they did not know, they wondered if he was killed. Job did not know where his family was either. He said to Christian and Joe, "I have found you and I am planning to escape Congo, so even if I do not have my own children, or know where they are, I cannot leave you. Your father was my pastor and I know you." So he took the boys with him as he was trying to escape. The three managed to travel together to Uganda.

Eventually Job arrived in Paidha with the boys. So he started asking people if anyone knew Kivi the father of these boys. Barnard said he knew Kivi and offered to take them to our home. I was so happy when they arrived. I did not have any food for them, so Barnard went out and found two pieces of corn. I prayed over that corn, and gave it to them along with some water to drink. I did not have any water for them to bathe, so they went to bed just as they were. When they arrived they were in bad health with rashes all over their bodies. But we prayed and thanked God. The next day our friends and neighbours came to see our children.

K: When I returned back home, I was so happy to see the boys. We cried and cried because they were alive. We were so thankful to Job for how he helped our boys. We last saw Job just before coming to Canada in 2007. He was still living the refugee life in Uganda. He had recently found his family – all but his eldest son, who was still missing. He and his family had been separated for about seven years.

We still had a number of problems to overcome. We had no documents or personal papers; we were living in Uganda illegally. At that time we were not even recognized as refugees. Paidha was only a small village so it had no United Nations High Commissioner for Refugees (UNHCR) office or refugee camp. We knew it would be best to go to Uganda's capital Kampala, to be registered with UNHCR there and to live in the refugee camp. But how to get there? It was 450 kilometres away. We had no money for anything, especially not for travel, and we did not know the local language. I did not know how to begin.

One day, our friend Barnard suggested I travel with him to a church in Bombo, another village farther away. I would watch him preach there. This man was a really good friend to us. When we arrived, he gave me the opportunity to preach in his place. After I finished, the members felt blessed. They asked if I would come to Bombo and help them with their preaching because they could see I was a man of God. It was also my desire, because Bombo was only thirty kilometres from the capital city of Kampala, and I knew we would be much closer to the UNHCR. When the church proposed I come, I told them I had a big family and could not come alone. I said I had one condition – that the church transport us to Bombo and provide us with a place to live. I said, "That is enough. Even if there is no food, I know that the God who cared for us in Paidha will care for us in Bombo." I knew that the relations we would create with the people there would help us provide, and we would be okay.

After one year in Bombo, the church leaders said they could not continue to offer me work. Our family was too big a financial burden for the size of the church. It was the church's custom to transport the pastor back to where he had come from. But I said that there was no sense in returning to Paidha; we needed to get to Kampala. The church was concerned with how we were going to live there. We felt we had no choice, as we were in a foreign country illegally and we needed to make a UNHCR claim. The church gave us money for three months of rent. We believed that God would provide the rest.

When we got to Kampala we could see that, again, everything was new for us. Our first question there was about what we needed to do to survive. We went right to the UNHCR offices to be registered. The UNHCR proposed that we live in the refugee camp, but we had another option. Another pastor friend at a church in Kampala, had said that if I helped at his church, the church would look after me and my family. The UNHCR agreed we could begin the paperwork for refugee status, but live outside the refugee camp, since living conditions inside were so difficult.

G: We lived in Kampala for four years, while waiting for our UNHCR claim to be completed.

The refugee life is a really hard life – no job, no money. You could want to work, but there were no jobs available.

K: I remember one time, my children were very small and we had no food. We spent three days without any food, nothing really. So the children started crying and I could see that they were in bad shape. I said, "Okay, come close; let us pray that God will provide some food." We prayed until the children fell asleep. But even though they were asleep, I said to Guilaine, "They will wake up and still they will need to eat." So I went out, but I did not know where to go. I just wandered around like a foolish man looking for food. When I finally returned, I was confused because Guilaine was preparing food.

G: While Kivi was out, someone came to our door. She had brought some things for us: two kilos of rice, oil, sugar and beans. I did not even know the woman. I said, "You do not even live close to us. How did you know about us?" She said, "Some people said someone new from Congo had arrived. I remember when Uganda was at war and I was living in

> The refugee life is a really hard life – no job, no money. You could want to work, but there were no jobs available.

Congo. I know the life of a refugee, so my heart pushed me to come and do something for you. I do not have much to give, but I want to share it with you and your family." A few weeks later someone else came knocking at the door, bringing a bag of food, saying, "This is not much, but let us share." That is how we survived.

Another time, the owner of our house came to ask for the rent money. We said we did not have the money at that time. After he left, we said, "Let us pray and see if we can find the money." For three or four months, the owner did not return. One day, friends arrived and said they had been thinking about us, and so they had come to visit and share the word of God. Later as they were leaving, they gave us an envelope and said they wanted to help us with some money for food. The very next day the owner of the house returned and asked for the rent money. We said we had it. That was a miracle.

K: As well, we were concerned because we could not afford to educate such a large number of children. School there is private and costs money. But our children needed an education or what would their futures be?

G: A woman spoke to me asking if all the children were ours, and why they were not studying. I said we did not have the money for school and uniforms. The woman asked me if I was a servant of God, and if I had faith. I said "Yes." She told me she was a teacher and she would speak to the principal of her school. The next day she returned and said, "Go and prepare your children, they will go to school." The school provided uniforms for our children, and let them go for free. We never paid anything.

K: How did we survive that time in Kampala? It is difficult to explain. Africa is not like Canada. In Canada, there are food banks and government assistance. There are things thrown away that can be re-used and there are a lot of people a good wish away who will help when they see others suffering. But not in Africa. Everyone is in need there. There may be a willingness to help, but people most often do not have enough to share. It was unbelievable to live all those years in Kampala without a job, and without money. We were living day to day. It is impossible to explain how we survived. It was a miracle.

G: There was just God, nothing else. Suffering as we did, we told the UNHCR we were considering going back to Congo. At least we had our own house there. I said to Kivi, "Let us go and die at home in Congo – not here." When the people at the UNHCR heard this, they could not understand why we would want to return. We said we had suffered a lot, life was so hard, and we were tired. We just needed to go back home. But the UNHCR said they could not allow us to return to DRC. It was not a safe solution. That was when we started to pray even harder and then to see the hand of God with the people coming to help us as we've explained.

K: Finally the UNHCR told us they thought it would be best for us to find a third country to live in. We thought that would be great. The UNHCR found that Canada would accept our application. The officers from Canada came to interview us. They heard our story and accepted our application. Another problem during our time in Kampala was that Christian needed surgery for a hernia, but we had no money to pay for his surgery and hospital stay. The UNHCR felt it would be best to get help for him once we got to Canada. As we waited for our travel visas to come, we

wondered what province we would live in and what our lives would be like there.

G: We arrived in wintertime. December. We had heard about the snow, but we did not know what it looked like. They said that in Canada it is cold, but we did not expect this kind of weather! We just knew it would be …

K: Cold!

G: When our plane arrived from Africa at the Toronto airport I was wearing a skirt, a sleeveless light T-shirt and flip flop sandals. Kivi was wearing shorts. At the arrivals gate we watched other people leaving the airport. We wanted to go outside and see the snow close up. We did not understand one word of English, but we understood the guards' actions that we could not leave the airport. We thought something must be wrong and we became afraid. We asked our children if they had done anything wrong and they said, "We didn't do anything!" Kivi and I wondered what could be the problem. So we said to each other, "Okay, let us wait, maybe there is something wrong with our papers." We sat for a very long time. Finally, the children were called into a room. I thought *Wow! What are they going to ask my children?*

I could not imagine. After a while the children came out with heavy jackets and boots on. I wondered why, because we did not know we would need this kind of clothing! Next they called Kivi and me into a room and gave us winter clothing too. Once we were all dressed we ran outside and everyone screamed NOOOOO! The kids came running back inside the airport saying "It's too cold to go outside! It's very, very cold!" I have never felt that kind of cold before. Living in Canada, we have laughed about the cold a lot!

K: When we first arrived in Winnipeg we stayed at Welcome Place, which assists refugees when they first arrive. They have programs to help newcomers get settled here. We also took the Entry Program. It was very helpful to orient us about things like Canadian laws, culture, transportation, shopping, and how to ask for assistance. When we looked for an apartment we went to the Immigrant and Refugee Community Organization of Manitoba (IRCOM) and met many people there. One woman invited us to her church. We were looking to join a Canadian church because we felt that would help us integrate more into the society here. We felt that if we worshipped with Canadians, we would learn English more quickly.

G: When I came here, I could not say anything in English, not even good morning. When people said "hi" to me, I did not know the meaning of the word. In Africa, people greet each other with "good morning." In my own country, "hi" is the Swahili word for garlic. We laughed a lot about our experiences of learning English.

> In my own country, "hi" is the Swahili word for garlic. We laughed a lot about our experiences of learning English.

K: The children are so quick to learn all the new things about Canada. There are many things Guilaine and I do not understand, and so we ask the kids. They help us with our problems and correct our English.

G: The kids will say "don't talk like *that*, talk like *this*." If they have homework, they must work together to help each other. It is very difficult for us to understand.

K: We still speak Swahili at home, to help our children remember it, but we don't know if they are getting it. They often do not reply, and we think they are just guessing at what we are saying. Guilaine and I are also interested in continuing to learn English, so they speak to us in English so we can practice.

The first time we got groceries, we rode the bus. We have a big family, so we needed lots of things. We were confused about how to transport our purchases. We had to take things from the shop to the bus stop, and then we had to take everything on the bus. It was all so heavy. And we put all our bags in the aisle of the bus. The people on the bus must have wondered what we were doing! It makes me laugh to remember.

G: And there were so many of us: nine people. It must have taken ten minutes just to get all of us and our things on the bus and pay.

K: We did not know so many things in the beginning.

G: Canada is good. In my country, people would have said, "Get off the bus, you are disturbing us."

K: Maybe the people here did say that, but we would not be able to understand what they were saying because we did not know the language! We have a very good Canadian friend, Sandy, who has become close to us. She was especially helpful in the early months, teaching us things and asking us what we needed. She began to drive us to get our groceries.

Fitting in is important, especially for our children. But as parents, we have a responsibility to them to examine what is good and not good. We have taught them that it's okay to want to fit in, but they cannot follow everything. We have to see which choices are appropriate and which are not, about things like clothing, behaving, speaking. The children are doing well.

We spent much of our lives in Congo, so it is hard to forget our traditions and cultures. When we arrived in Canada, things were a bit hard. But now we are here and mixing both cultures because this is a new way of life and Canada is now our home. The most important thing is that we are together.

The first step was to make a new start, and that has been a big challenge. But now I want more. Back home, as a pastor and a businessman, I was helping people in my community. But here, I feel that I am not doing anything special to make a difference.

My focus now is to improve my English and continue studying and taking courses while I work fulltime. I graduated from high school in 2012. I want to participate and do something to make a difference. If I am not doing anything for others I feel more stress. Helping others feels like a release.

G: I finished high school in 2012 too. I have to be patient and go step by step until I reach my goal. My dream is to be an early childcare assistant. People tell me I have excellent experience from raising my seven children.

K: We want our children to remember what God has done for us in our life. We want the children to always remember the assistance we received from strangers and how the Canadian government took care of us. We were unknown people. We want to teach our children to remember this and to be kind to others too.

I think it was God's plan that Guilaine and I married. Many people lose their marriages and families because of the hard times they have living the refugee life. After arriving in Canada, we found there were many families with problems and many couples that were separated. Maybe part of it is the stress of not having much money. For us, separation has never happened, and we do not think it will. We have already passed through the most difficult periods in our life and we are still together.

During our worst struggles in Uganda, I could see Guilaine was really suffering; she was sleeping on the floor, and we did not have enough food. I asked her if she wanted to leave me and go back to her family. I would try to get us a better life and call her to return.

G: But I said I could not do that because I married Kivi for better or for worse, not just to be married for the good times.

> My dream is to be an early childcare assistant. People tell me I have excellent experience from raising my seven children.

There was one question during the interview that Guilaine and Kivi could not answer. I asked them both how witnessing the amazing kindness of strangers as well as the unbelievable violence and hatred of people fighting had affected them? Silence was their answer.

Guilaine just shook her head quietly, her eyes drifting. Kivi looked up, his own eyes filled with tears and focused on something high up towards the ceiling. Finally, Guilaine spoke: "We do not want to cry, instead we want to thank God because we were helped." As with any of the refugees I have interviewed, I wonder what they have lived through, but kept private – those things too personal, too deeply felt to share.

SIERRA LEONE

SALLY

I am a link in an empowering chain.
If those before me could do it, so can I, and if I can do it,
so can all the others who come after me.

My sister came to Canada before me, in the 1980s. She lives in Toronto now, but when I was leaving Sierra Leone she said, "Don't start out in Toronto; go to Winnipeg. It will be horribly cold, but the people are friendly and it will see you through." Not only has Winnipeg seen me through, it has welcomed me and sustained me.

I arrived with very little and there were many of us: my daughter and me as well as my elderly mom and three of her other grand-children. When we first arrived, I quickly found a church to attend. It was difficult for me, but I stood up in church and said, "I have come to Canada and I have nothing." Initially it was hard for me to ask because it is not a custom in my culture to ask for assistance. I was honest because I needed the help. I love Canadians; they are respectful, and they want to be helpful. If you ask they will give you more than you need. That first day at church, Gerry and Frank came forward to help me. They became my Canadian mom and dad, coming over often to help with such things as hanging curtains or delivering a mattress. I'm used to a very large and close extended family back in Sierra Leone, so it felt good to make room in my new life for these people.

I came to Canada because I had been living surrounded by war and had seen the suffering up close. My mother, then in her late sixties, had to hide in the rural bush of Sierra Leone for two months to protect her three young grandchildren. Our country was not safe. We had family members die, and so we decided to get out. That was 2002.

Today, I am part of a community, one I am proud to say many of us have built together – the Central Park neighbourhood. Sure there are drug dealers and crime here, but there are many strengths too. People here open their doors and their hearts to each other. That is the way to survive as a newcomer. About seventy-five percent of the people in our community are refugees or immigrants, and we take pride in our neighbourhood. Each spring, we hold a cleanup and BBQ across the street at Central Park. There is so much good here. The park comes alive in the summer months. A few years ago, we got the idea to create a marketplace just like the ones back home. Now Fridays and Saturdays in the warm months, we come together, selling things we have made or grown, and performing drama and displaying our arts. As well, we are selling the crops from our co-operative garden.

To me, community means everybody coming together – children, mothers, fathers – all of us giving, sharing, supporting and putting our resources together to help each other out. I like working in community.

Canada is a strange country for refugees. So many things are different here – the weather, the language, the food, the culture. Adjusting to these changes is difficult. So we need to ask ourselves, how can we help each other? How can we sustain each other? Let us take into account our beliefs, our values, and let us respect each other. That is community.

It is my joy to help others. I work as a Community Development Coordinator. I don't spend much time in my office; I go out

> People here open their doors and their hearts to each other. That is the way to survive as a newcomer.

to be with the people. I believe that as human beings, we should be ready to help others who are less privileged than we are. From the time I was a small child, I have always believed this. If a baby fell down, I would be the one to run and pick it up. I always had followers. My mother said, "You are always around people; people feel comfortable around you." Yes, I do find it easy to be with people. I am an extrovert. It makes me feel good to help the suffering and vulnerable, and to empower the women.

Where I come from, women don't have rights: they can't speak out or make political decisions. They don't even have the ultimate right to their own bodies, so if they are abused or raped there is no way for them to seek help or justice. It is only now that women in Africa are fighting for their rights and to be able to have representation in decision making. That is very new in our society. Women need help to know what their rights are. If a woman is abused, here in Canada you dial 911, but that service does not exist in Africa. There is no point in going to the police there, for who are the police? Men. There lies the bias, and this bias is part of the system already. Living here in Canada, my

message to my newcomer sisters is, *Come, see your strengths and see what you can do.* Empowerment to me comes from within. It is awareness. It means taking control over your life, equipping yourself, making yourself who you want to be. This is my message to the women here.

Everyday my office doors are open. We've started a sewing co-operative, a conversational English group, and we are gardening on land given to us by the University of Manitoba. On Fridays, we take turns cooking our native foods for each other because we are a diverse group: Somali, Ethiopian, Korean, Sierra Leonean, Sudanese, Liberian, Filipino, Aboriginal, Nigerian, South American and Chilean. I offer my office area to my Muslim friends so they have a space to pray each day. We respect each other.

In May 2009, I graduated from the University of Manitoba with my social work degree. I was so happy that all the hard work was over and I had reached my goal for now. I have also received a diploma in nursing from Sierra Leone, another diploma in Secretarial Science and a three-year degree in accounting from a school in Liberia, but none of this was recognized in Canada. I was devastated by this, but I continued on and went back to school part time. I did not receive any student loans because I was ineligible. A single woman with grown children is not granted a student loan the same way a younger single woman is. Instead, I worked full time supporting my family, while going to university as well.

Education is very important to me. Education to a newcomer means advancement and added empowerment, although empowerment comes first from within. I was so disappointed when my first degree was not honoured; it was a slap in the face. It cost me so much money. I have had to work two and three jobs just to go to school. Newcomers whose education is not accepted in Canada have a hard time. They take on menial jobs to pay for their re-education because with no valid education they can easily go down the drain. It is difficult to advance. I know how hard it is for these refugees.

When I graduated, my friends had a surprise party for me. It was wonderful. Someday I want to celebrate by leading an empowerment forum for young women. It is the youth I really want to reach. My message to them is, *Look at me, I am fifty-seven. If I can do this, others can do it too.* I get the strength to be resilient from knowing about all the people who have succeeded before me, people who have struggled to receive their education, gained independence and are forging ahead. I am a link in an empowering chain. If those before me could do it, so can I, and if I can do it, so can all the others who come after me. This is my message.

When I was young, I lived with my aunties. They beat me and told me I was good for nothing. I felt so low I tuned my mind to accept the beatings; it was part of my daily life. But the only thing I never accepted was that I was good for nothing and couldn't do anything with my life. I said to myself, *I will take these beatings, but I will do something with my life, and I will impart this message to other women. I will stand for the truth, for what I believe in, and not accept what these other people are telling me.*

I plan to take this message back to Sierra Leone. My hope is that, in ten years, I will

> Education to a newcomer means advancement and added empowerment, although empowerment comes first from within.

have a resource centre there. It will be for every woman and girl-child of Sierra Leone. I have a special place in my heart for these less fortunate girls. They are young and not in school. Often they have no parents, having been orphaned by war or AIDS. They are in need and have no way to cope. I want to teach them they can rise above the abuse and the suffering; they can find their voice and become strong. I want to empower women and the girl-child to give them hope in society. I want to help women know how to live their lives independent of men.

I love Canada. My family will stay, but I will sacrifice what I have made for myself here, in order to return to my country and change the people. My ex-husband used to laugh at me and say sarcastically, "You want to change the world?!" But I will, empowering women, one at a time.

The first time I met Sally, I came with a guest as a last minute tag-along to a community lunch she was hosting. But she welcomed us in as she would a good friend. She said it is the African way to welcome extra people. Her big-heartedness proved itself again the day I asked her if she had any suggestions for individuals who could be interviewed for this book. She offered herself. A woman who is constantly giving, she was the first person to offer her story, and I am very grateful to her.

CHRIS

You never get to know people until you interact personally.
We presume people are all the same.

I was born in Liberia in 1982, one brother with five sisters. As the only son, I want to represent my family and tell our experiences of moving from Liberia to Ghana and then to rural Manitoba. By telling our story, I also want to honour my mom, Lucy, and especially my dad – not my biological dad, Peter, who died before I could get to know him when I was just a boy, but my Mom's second husband, Sartu, who raised us and is the man I choose to call father.

My older sisters Rose and Agnes are deceased, then there's Victoria, me, and after me, Christiana and Justina. Our family lived close to the border of Liberia and Cote d'Ivoire. My biological dad worked for the Liberian government, and when he heard news that the civil war was coming to our area, we moved to Monrovia, the capital of Liberia located on the coast of the Atlantic Ocean. My dad thought the rebels would not yet have reached Monrovia. This war was an ethnic crisis and my parents were each from rival tribes that were at loggerheads. Keeping our parents together and safe was a serious problem. We knew our family was at risk. Eventually this ethnic crisis reached Monrovia too. My dad's tribe wanted my mother turned over to them. My father could have done this and just walked away, but he refused. He would rather have been killed by his own tribe than allow them to kill my mom and bring harm to my sisters and me. It is likely that had we not escaped, my sisters would have been raped and I would have been forced to become a child soldier. So that's how we lost my biological dad in 1990.

We stayed in Monrovia from 1990 to 1996. It was really bad: no government, rebels in town, people being killed. There was little access to food and clean drinking water. In 1996, the country was divided, but there was a ceasefire. That's when my mom met Sartu – the man I call my dad. He was working for the Liberian Electricity Corporation making some money. He decided to take up the responsibility of our family and marry my mom. My mom and Sartu were from the same tribe. Violence was increasing and there was talk of a second civil war. Sartu knew that their tribe would be targeted. He said he was not going to allow more violence to happen to my mother and us children. So he started to make a plan to escape the country. While in the process, someone hinted to my parents that they were being watched closely; people from another tribe were checking up on our house three to four times a week just to make sure we were still around. If the ceasefire did not hold, my family would be a target.

My dad talked to one of his Nigerian friends who had a boat and agreed to help us escape. So one night at about 2:00 in the morning, this friend knocked on the door and we left immediately. We took everything with us that we could carry. The boat was a fishing boat meant to hold about twenty people, but it was leaking and in need of repair. Our belongings were too heavy and the boat started to sink. We had to throw things into the water, things we later wished we could have saved like bar soap and laundry soap. We threw so much into the water, that we basically had nothing left, not even food or drinking water. We had to bail water out of the boat the whole four days we

> We had to bail water out of the boat the whole four days we were on the water.

were on the water. I think it was November 1999. We travelled northwest to the country of Guinea. Unfortunately, they did not allow us entry into the country. The officials said Guinea was not taking any Liberian refugees because the civil war was senseless. They felt there was no reason for Liberians to be killing their own people. All of this was very upsetting. We got back on the boat and travelled back past Liberia and on to Ghana, which is east of Liberia and the neighbouring country of Cote d'Ivoire. We did not stop at Cote d'Ivoire because it was a French-speaking country and we spoke no French and also because we knew they had strict rules for visitors. We were happy when we reached Ghana and were accepted, but that is just the beginning of our story.

Once accepted, we were taken to the Buduburam refugee camp, the largest refugee camp in western Africa. There were about 40,000 people living there. The camp was very congested. The United Nations High Commissioner for Refugees (UNHCR) no longer had resources for new refugees because in 1990 when the civil war in Liberia first started, 25,000 to 30,000 people made up the first group to leave for Ghana. All the resources were spent on them. When we arrived, we were given only basic food for a few days. We had nowhere to stay, so we just stayed outside in an open field close to the refugee camp. We had no mosquito nets, so malaria was a big concern. Two of my sisters, Rose and Agnes, contracted malaria and died three weeks later.

After three weeks of us sitting outdoors like that, the UNHCR took us to live in a school. They had to stop children from going to classes so that they had a place to keep the refugees. We claimed a little spot with some desks and chairs. There were twenty-six or twenty-seven classrooms and still they couldn't fit everyone there. There was no sanitation; refugees were relieving themselves everywhere so there was also cholera and diarrhea. People died in numbers, at least eight a day, every day for six months.

Throughout the conflicts in Liberia, I had tried to go to school. Whenever there was a cease-fire and it was safer, I would go back. I was able to complete my schooling to Grade 12 before moving to Ghana. I was thankful for this because when I got there I was given the opportunity by the UNHCR to go to a nursing school in the city of Accra five hours away.

The UNHCR wanted to train Liberians to help their refugee community. It was a fast-track program. We went for three-week periods at a time and then would stay in Buduburam in between. My first priority was my family, and I felt that with this opportunity to live in the city would come food and, hopefully, a chance to meet different people who could help us. I thought maybe once I got to know people there, I could bring my family to Accra. Initially, that was my plan, but when I got there it was totally different. Unfortunately for us, the Ghanaians did not understand us refugees. They thought we were all just bad people who fled our country because all we wanted to do was kill our brothers. We felt very misunderstood and unaccepted.

I had two Liberian friends at school and we talked about this lack of understanding. We felt the Ghanaians were not educated about what refugee life was like. They just didn't understand. We thought that although they saw us differently, we should help them to know us better. At lunch hour in the cafeteria, the Liberian and Ghanaian students sat at separate tables with no interaction. So my friends and I made a plan. One lunch hour we hurried ahead to the cafeteria and bought all of the food there. It was a small cafeteria, but we did not have much money and so it took all of our savings to do this. When the Ghanaians came for lunch there was no food left. They could not understand why there was no food and when they asked the cafeteria worker, she told them that the Liberians had bought it all. We went to them and invited them to come and eat with us. We told them we had already paid for it all. They sat with us and got to know us. We told them about why we had fled Liberia and explained that we were just people who didn't want to be killed. They really appreciated my story about the way I lost my biological dad and about the courage my new dad took to help my family. When they knew my story, they told me that I had been through a lot and they were impressed that I chose to go to school and continue living as I was. They said, "We have to put our hands around Chris."

Once we explained our stories, that really changed things. You never get to know people until you interact personally. We presume people are all the same. We all started to become friends. Later, once we graduated from nursing school, some of our Ghanaian friends came back to the refugee camp to work with us. They didn't even get paid; they volunteered their services. In fact, one of my Ghanaian friends, Julius, even went on to move to Liberia and work there.

The whole of 2000, I travelled back and forth from the refugee camp to Accra for school. After I completed my studies, I had the opportunity to work at the UNHCR hospital on the refugee camp with some Ghanaian doctors. I was a physician's assistant. I admitted patients and looked after them and also helped physicians with the medications. The pay is very small – about $2 a month – so I was really a volunteer. But you must understand that the work was not so much about the pay, but about access to things. Everything for the refugee camp is distributed from hospitals: food, water and medication. It was a big benefit to receive some access to these things. My priority was not the money but looking after my family. With the bit of money I made, I built a little three-room shelter. The sides were brick and the roof was zinc metal. On the refugee camp property people began to settle, building shelters and taking up farming.

Our family's immigration to Canada began with my cousin Henry. He was

sponsored and came to rural Manitoba and then began an application to try to sponsor his seven siblings to come as well. They were older orphans in their twenties but felt they could not apply to come on their own and needed a guardian. They knew that if a group of young men and women applied for asylum and had no parents they could be discriminated against. Once again, the Ghanaians did not really understand the problems in Liberia and young Liberians alone could be viewed as potential rebels trying to get a free ride to Canada. Henry felt that in order for his family to be successfully accepted they needed to find an older person to be part of the application. So he called my mom, who is their aunt, and asked her and my dad to consider applying for them all.

It was a tough decision. Initially, my mom and dad refused. They did not feel that, considering everything we had been through as a family, they could take Henry's siblings to Canada and leave the rest of us children back in Ghana. But we knew our parents would not forget about us and then a few other things helped to convince our parents to take the chance and go. As well, at that time, I was working and we had access to food. We were doing relatively okay. So my mom and dad went for the interview about sponsoring my seven cousins. They were approved and their visas were issued. They were all sponsored to go to Holland, Manitoba, a small town close to Winkler. The night before my mom and dad left, my God we wept.

My mom and dad arrived in Canada in 2004. They were so upset that they could not eat. There was so much food in Canada and they had no way to get it back to us. For days, they did not eat, but they didn't say why. Their sponsors were a couple who had two adult daughters. One named Suzanne lived in a town close by and came to visit often. She tried to find out what was troubling my mom – if you see somebody stressed out, you can generally tell. Finally my mom opened up to Suzanne and told her about her family back in Ghana and why she could not eat. Suzanne assured my mom and then promised her that she would try to bring us children to Canada. My parents did not take her words seriously. They just couldn't believe that was possible.

My mom also told Suzanne that she really wanted to go to church because back home she went every Sunday. They did not drive and there was no church within walking distance so they had not been able to go. She asked Suzanne to help her find a Pentecostal church. The pastor of the Pentecostal church that Suzanne took my mother to was named Robert White. Suzanne introduced my mom to this pastor and he took an interest in her and our family's story. He also felt committed to helping Suzanne get us kids to Canada. Suzanne and Robert began the process of private sponsorship. Six churches in the Carmen area came together one after the other to help us: two United Churches, two Pentecostal, one Mennonite and one Catholic. The connection was amazing. They called their group Christians helping Christians.

One day, I received an email from a woman named Tracy saying she had sent me $1000 and giving me the reference number for a Western Union transfer. I laughed and thought it was an email scam. I did not bother to look into it. At the camp, a family of five could live comfortably on $50 a month. This would buy food, clean drinking water and there would even be some money left over to buy clothes. Then another email came about an offer of money. Again, I did not answer it. I talked with my sisters about it, but we thought it was too good to be true. Finally, my mom telephoned and asked me if I was getting the money. Tracy was one of the women from the church group. First I emailed her back and said she must have made a mistake by adding an extra zero to $100. I was wrong. Imagine us getting $1,000! No banks use US or Canadian money because of security, so they would pay us in Ghanaian Cedi currency. This $1,000 would be a bag full of money! I thought, *even if I go and get this money how would I ever bring it home?*

I called a taxi. Even the taxi drivers are not to be trusted, so I took three separate taxis to get to the bank. I took the first taxi to the other side of the city and had it drop me off. Then the next taxi driver dropped me down town, and so on. From there, I walked a while and went into the bank. The money fit into one and a half large garbage bags. The bags were black so no one could see inside. I had to double the bags because the money was so heavy. I then walked maybe four blocks from the bank and took the first of three taxis back home the same way I had come. I was not afraid because who would ever think that a guy like me, dressed the way I was, would ever carry that much money. (It was easy to spot that I was a refugee and not a Ghanaian – my clothes were very simple, I was dirty and dusty and I looked poor.) Still, I could not believe what was happening. I felt like I was in a dream, until I got back home and we realized, *we have the money.*

We could not tell anyone. We had no lock on our door – there aren't any in a refugee camp. We thought about one of us staying home all the time, but we knew people would wonder what was going on. So we just left the money in the open house and went on living our normal lives. But it didn't stop there, because the church group started sending us $300 a month. $300 *every* month! Plus Suzanne sent me additional money to get our documents. My sisters were shocked that people who did not know us would help. This money we received was life changing. We had excess food; our house was filled. We even had new clothes. Things changed dramatically for us. We then had a luxurious life. You could see the changes so we had to explain to people that we had assistance from sponsors. We did not say how

> My sisters were shocked that people who did not know us would help.

much money though. The money didn't help only us; it helped others too. We would stockpile food and our friends and neighbours would come to take some. It gave us the ability to share and help others.

As we prepared our applications for Canada, we were advised by the Canadian consulate in Ghana that because we were so many people – myself, my three sisters, my sister Victoria's two children and my late sister Agnes's two children – we should split up the group into two applications. If one was denied, the other would hopefully get accepted. Or, if someone in our group were to get a communicable disease (say tuberculosis) then our entire group would not be further delayed. Justina, Christiana and I made one application and my sister Victoria and the four children made another. I was the principle applicant for my group.

Sometimes things happen and we don't ever know why. The man who interviewed me at the Canadian Consulate had studied medicine in Newfoundland, so when he asked me about what I did for a living, we got talking. I showed him newspaper articles I had as evidence of my work with the UNHCR and refugees. He said that he knew about my story and after reading our file, he could see there would be huge support for us from Canada. He told me that if we passed the medicals he would issue our visas. That was it. He asked only two questions during the whole interview. He sent me out, and my sister Victoria was called in. She went in alone, and the four children waited outside because that's how they do it. At the end of the hour, he said you are all successful, just go and do your medicals. But for some reason, I was issued the medical papers for myself and my two sisters but Victoria was not given any that same day. We didn't feel we could ask questions and we were unsure what to do. We presumed the papers would come soon, so we went home.

We did our medicals and before Victoria even received her medical request slips, we had our visas issued and were set to leave. It took one year for Victoria to get those papers. We do not know why this happened. When she finally got them, it took another eight months to get their medical results. She had to go for a follow-up medical, and then finally she passed. Justina, Christiana and I arrived in Canada in July 2007.

As we were waiting to come to Canada in April, my mom called and told me my dad was diagnosed with cancer. It was serious and the doctors could not do anything to help. I did not take this seriously. When I considered everything my family had been through – surviving the conflict in Liberia and living in the refugee camp in Ghana – I thought it would not be possible in the country of Canada with all its capabilities, for there to be nothing that could be done to help my dad. I remained very positive. I thought God would help and my dad would get through it. I felt that once I got to Canada and actually saw my family, I'd be able to better understand what was going on.

I saw the change at the airport when they came to meet us; physically my dad was a completely different person than when I had last seen him in Ghana. He had lost a lot of weight. I do not have a brother, so my dad was everything to me. But after some time to think about everything, I came to the conclusion that even if my dad passed away, at least my mom would be close by me. If I showed some form of depression, who was going to help my mom? I decided I had to have composure so I could help her and talk to her. I needed to tell her everything would be okay.

About two months after arriving, my dad took me for a walk one day and he began to talk about life. He told me to always work hard, to earn my money right and to never cheat. He said, "be honest with people." He told me that where you start is not as important as where you finish. My dad asked me not to smoke because he said that if you smoke, that will lead to buying weed and the cops would be watching for that. He said the next thing you know, your life will be ruined. I asked him why he was telling me all these things and he said, "I am just telling you how life is. One day you'll have a family of your own." Then he took me to a Canadian Tire store. He showed me a few scooters for old people and he said that was what he had been thinking of getting for my mom when she was sixty-two or sixty-three because her knees hurt. He asked me to make sure I bought a scooter for my mom. I asked, "What about you?" But he just laughed. Then we drove through a cemetery and he asked me "Can you imagine people dying here in the winter, with ice and snow falling on their graves?" I told him that once people are dead they're dead. I don't think they'd know what was going on. He said, "You might think they don't know, but it's freezing cold!" We just laughed. And then he told me he wanted to be buried in

Africa. I said, "Okay, it's your call, but not right now because we don't have money and we've still got some doctors to consult."

The next day Suzanne said to me "Your father wants to go back to Africa and help with Victoria and his grandchildren's delayed visas." But I still did not believe he would go back to Africa. My mom told me that the doctor had said his time was getting closer. My dad said that the best way he could make my late sister Agnes happy wherever she was, was to make sure her two children came to Canada. He was persistent. He talked to Suzanne and the church group constantly. He told them he had to go ... and he did.

He called us once he was back at Buduburam. He was happy to be with Victoria and the children. He took them to the Canadian Consulate in Ghana for meetings and asked the people there to help his family. He felt he was making a difference. One week and three days after arriving back in Ghana, he died. He is buried at the refugee camp. Victoria and the children eventually arrived in Winkler in January 2009.

I was happy to be reunited with my family, but it took me some time to get settled. I felt very nurtured by the church group that sponsored us. So many people kept coming around to meet us and bring us gifts. I knew they were doing that to be generous, but it was too much for me. I wasn't used to that.

The rural area of Manitoba where we lived was not multi-ethnic. There was one black family living in Morden and just one black person living in Winkler. But I did not mind. One day, I went to the small town of Plum Coulee close by, and an older lady stopped me on the street and held my hand. She said she had never touched a black person before. I just laughed and laughed. She asked me where I was from and I told her a bit about myself. She said she wished she could sponsor an African. I told her that I had many friends back in Ghana she could help if she wanted. She asked for one friend's phone number. She did not sponsor him, but she sent him some money.

Unfortunately, most immigrants do not stay in rural Manitoba for long. There is no access to post-secondary education. Another

> ... an older lady stopped me on the street and held my hand. She said she had never touched a black person before. I just laughed and laughed.

important reason people leave is that there is no access to traditional African food. We had to travel to Winnipeg to find a special store with some of the foods we liked. And then there is the cold. My cousin, Henry, felt it was too cold in Manitoba, so he moved to Nova Scotia. (Later on, he wanted to move to a place where you could make more money so he moved again, this time to Calgary.)

I lived in rural Manitoba until December 2008. Christiana and Justina moved to Winnipeg first, and then I too had to make the decision to leave my mom. University was a priority. My mom understood. She told me that if I wanted to go to school, I would have to go to Winnipeg. She said to me "You've got to carry on with your life. You can't be around me all the time." Today, I am a conflict resolution major at the University of Winnipeg, and also work full time. I play competitive soccer and my teammates are great. I have made a lot of friends in Winnipeg, so it feels more like home now.

Victoria moved to Montreal with her two children and recently my mom and my deceased sister Agnes's two children moved to Montreal to be with them. My mom's greatest joy comes from the lives of her children and grandchildren. We all have good character: we've never been arrested, and we work hard. We live in a free society where we are not discriminated against. We do not have to struggle for anything. We can get whatever we want. She has said to me that she does not fear death anymore because she has seen so much and then also she's got a whole lot of family to see when she dies.

I felt like I was leaving opportunity when I moved into Winnipeg, because I was leaving all my sponsors. Words are very inadequate for me to describe how I feel about them. They are very good people. Godsent. One sponsor Robert White feels like not only my pastor, but my friend and brother. A number of sponsors have said if I need anything, *anything*, I can just call them. Even years later, they continue to stand by me. But I do not want to be dependent. I must carry on with my own life. I need to go out and make my own money.

In 2010, I returned to Buduburam for a visit. I went to my dad's grave and cleaned and decorated it. When I stood at his grave, I thought about what he had said to me when he was alive: that where you start is not as important as where you finish. I thought about how he supported us through the war

in 1996 when we really needed help. He also did his best at the end of his life by helping us. When I think about his comment in retrospect, and I think about what we all went through and how he lived his life helping us and loving us right up until the end, I think he died a happy man.

During my visit to Ghana, I thought I would be sad at the condition of the refugee camp and my friends' lives, but I did not feel downhearted. One reason was that I had brought some money to share. I bought lots of water and just gave it away to about a hundred people. At least they had water for two or three days. And I gave a woman money to cook for my friends and me. We sat around together and ate and talked about life. I noticed how comfortable people can be in poverty. They don't have so many things, but they are happy. Their attitudes encouraged me a lot.

I compare that to what people have here in Canada. We have so much and yet we complain. But I think for Canadians, this is only what they know. They haven't seen anything else. In Ghana, just eating isn't so bad. When I lived there, I weighed 120 pounds. Now I weigh 180 and I am not overweight. The average Canadian sees so many things here to want. Most people have their own cars. If others have a car, and one person doesn't, that person gets stressed. It's like being below society's standard. The typical person in Canada will also have a job. If you don't have one, you can't afford to do anything. But over in Ghana, most people don't have jobs. They don't have a choice and because they don't have a choice they accept that. That's their life. If all you know is the refugee life, then there is very little expectation for anything better.

There are lots of people who still need help, especially those in the refugee camps. I always tell people that it is not over yet. The fact that some of us were fortunate to come here is not the end; it is only the beginning. If some of the refugees in the camps were to tell their stories to you, you'd say, "You know, Chris's story is nothing. There are worse hardships."

When I open my book of life, and I look through it, I see all kinds of experiences. Good has come from all parts, even the unlucky ones. Everything in my life has turned out for the better; that's how I see it. Had all those things not happened in my life, I would not be where I am today. If I had not lived through the war in Liberia, I would not have gone to Ghana. If my mom had not left Ghana, I would not have ended up here in Canada. Everything that happened has turned out to be fortunate for me. People would say my dad passing away was very bad and unlucky. But what has that taught me? It has taught me to be responsible and very independent. And most importantly, to get regular medical checkups. It has taught me about life.

My dad taught me difficult times don't last forever. He said never worry about tomorrow; tomorrow will take care of its self. There is always a better day.

While Chris was living at the Buduburam camp he met a Canadian woman named Karen volunteering at the camp. She left a strong impression on him. She told him that Canadians were good people and the country had so much to share. She said she wished she could take everybody from the camp back there. This gave Chris a very hopeful feeling about Canada and brought him great confidence when decisions were being made about his parents' future and the family's separation. Chris says he feels everything happens for a reason; everything is part of a greater plan.

RAQIYA

I was raised to be an independent, strong woman.

In 1991, the civil war began in Somalia. Violence between tribes stopped all government control and changed everything. I am from a small tribe called the Asharaf. We are religious people who were respected in Somalia, but now, no one respects anyone. I lost everything because of the civil war; it was all taken from me, even my house. And I was separated from my children for almost ten years. That was the worst. Thank God we have been reunited.

I was born in Mogadishu, the capital city of Somalia. Somalis don't celebrate birthdays or keep track of them like Canadians do, so I don't know the exact date, but I know I was born around 1938 and so I say I am seventy-five. My mother died when I was eight, so I became very close with my father. He married a woman who treated me well and I had a really good life as a child. I had eleven siblings in total: my biological mother had eight children including me (three with a previous husband who died, and five with my father) and then my second mother had four children. Of the twelve, only five of us survived to become adults; the other seven passed away from illnesses as children.

I did not go to school when I was a child, which was not that common in Somali at the time. In the 1940s, most kids went to Arabic school or Italian school (Somalia had been colonized by Italy) and almost all the kids went to Koran classes, but I was very active and also a bit difficult, so my dad said I must stay home. (I have changed and am now calm as an adult.) Also, after my mother died, there was a lot of work to be done and I was the eldest daughter. I did housework and cooked for my family.

When I was seventeen, my father arranged for me to marry a man I had never met. We had three children and now there are also twelve grandchildren and four great grandchildren. My husband died from an illness around 1989 before the civil war began.

I have always worked, even when my husband was alive. I was raised to be an independent, strong woman. I've never just sat around somewhere waiting for others to serve me. I worked hard for my family at home when I was a girl, and I have been a wholesaler, a volunteer teacher and a midwife. Of the three jobs, I liked delivering babies the best.

When I was a teenager, I used to watch the midwives delivering my sisters-in-law's babies. In Somalia, most people do not go to the hospital to deliver a baby, but call the midwife to come to your home. One day, when I was about eighteen, I was staying with a woman and the baby was ready to come but the midwife had not arrived yet, so I delivered the baby myself. I did not know what to do with the baby's umbilical cord. I wanted to pull it out, but I left it there! When the midwife arrived she showed me how to cut it. This first baby I delivered was a boy named Mahamud Hassan. I got a lot of hands-on experience in the community and so I started volunteering as a midwife. People would knock on my door in the middle of the night to take me to a house where a woman was ready to give birth.

Getting an education was important to me. I started school after I had my three children, when I was around thirty-five. I went to Italian and Arabic classes because at that time those were the languages used in my country. I had not learned as a child to read the Koran,

Getting an education was important to me. I started school after I had my three children, when I was around thirty-five.

which is the holy Muslim book written in Arabic, so I learned to read it as an adult. In 1960, Somalia gained its independence. The written Somali language did not start until 1972. Because the Somali language uses the English Latin alphabet (the same as Italian) I already knew my alphabet. The Somali language is written the way it sounds, so it's easy to learn once you know the alphabet. In 1972, I went to Somali classes once a week and then the Somali government asked me to teach other Somalis our new written language. The literacy rate was very low so the government spent a lot of money to educate the Somali people. I used to travel to nomadic villages to teach both adults and children. The country's literacy rate improved to something like seventy percent. At that same time, I also worked for the City of Mogadishu sewing uniforms for schools and soldiers.

But then around 1973, I got offered good training in a hospital to become a midwife. A gentleman who lived in the neighbourhood and worked for the government had come to see me. He asked if I'd had any training. When I said no, he offered to register me with the city. My training was at the well-known hospital in Mogadishu, called Martini. I

spent six months working there and then they gave me a certificate and all the equipment I would need to be a midwife. The next year, I opened my own place to deliver babies in my house. I had two rooms: one for delivering the babies and one for the mothers to stay in and rest afterwards. I let anyone who had no one to help them back home stay three days; otherwise the women would go home right away. If there was an emergency or something was not right (like the feet coming first), I would take the mother to the hospital. There were not many cars, so people took taxis to the hospital. Some women even came to me in wheelbarrows with their legs up. I did not charge a fee, but people would give me money or things to thank me. If anyone was really poor and didn't have the money to take a taxi, I would pay for their taxi home. I knew I would get my rewards from God. I have delivered eight of my grandchildren: Mustafa, Anissa, Fahima, Raqiya, Sadea and Mohammed (who are both deceased), Safa and Fatuma.

I received a lot of respect for being a midwife. That very first boy I delivered – Mahamud Hassan – worked with me when I had a job sewing uniforms for the government in about 1972. I was expected to sew thirty pairs of pants each day. The young man was very fast and so when he was done his pants, he would come to me and take some of mine to help me finish. Everyone in the community knew me and called me *hooyo*, which means mom. I received that kind of respect because I was doing something good for the community.

Besides being a midwife, I had a shop (like a convenience store) in my home where I sold food and basic necessities. When I was not busy delivering babies, I would open my shop. After my husband passed away, around 1989, besides having my little store and midwifery clinic, I also travelled to other countries like Yemen to buy clothes. I would bring them back, and my son would sell them to the storeowners in Mogadishu.

One day years later, another young man I had delivered put a gun to my chest in an act of violence. He was a *jiri* – a Somali word used for a militiaman or anyone who chooses to carry a gun. In 1991, there was no government and guns were everywhere, especially for the young people. This young man did not like my tribe. I had just gone to see my neighbour, who was from another tribe, to get something I had lent her. She was not home, but her door was unlocked and as I came out the door of her house a young guy with a gun called me over and asked me what tribe I was from. I said Asharaf. He and his group would not believe me. Just then, my neighbour came back and called my name "Sharifo Raqiya." In my culture, this is a respectful way of saying *hello Raqiya of the Asharaf tribe*. The guy was confused and argued with the neighbour saying that I was not Asharaf. The neighbour called out to him "What, you guys can't read? Look at the sign on her door it says *Sharifo Raqiya – midwife*." The guy paused, made a face and said "Oh no!" The gunman said he remembered coming to my house when it looked different – before it was fixed up and had a new gate. He had come with his mom and pregnant sister. I delivered his sister's baby. From this, he realized I had also delivered him, but at the hospital. If you are delivered at the hospital, the midwife's name is written on the birth certificate. He backed off immediately, taking the gun from my chest as soon as he

> One day years later, another young man I had delivered put a gun to my chest in an act of violence.

realized all this. He kept saying over and over "Forgive me. I am so sorry I have done this." I said to him "Ask forgiveness of God."

There was so much violence in our area of Mogadishu at that time. The militia came to my older brother's house and opened a machine gun on everyone. His wife and oldest son, then seventeen, were killed. My brother was shot at too, but somehow he and his two daughters survived. They all ran away and let the militia take everything. At that time, I was a widow and I took my kids and fled to another, safer area of the city. We moved around a lot trying to get away from the gunfire and explosions. We would run and stay in a camp or shack in a safer area and then when that area became violent, we'd flee again. In Somali tradition, we do not have wedding rings, but men will buy very nice jewelry for their women. During the war, jewellery was the easiest things to carry. We would sell it to survive. I sold all the jewelry I had so I could buy food for my family. We had to start over many times. Looking around Mogadishu now you can see the whole city has been destroyed by the violence.

One day, I returned to my old house to see if anything such as blankets were left that I

could take with me. As I was walking up the street, I saw there was an old truck with the roof cut off and a machine gun coming out of where the roof had been in the passenger area. We call these *technical vehicles*. People were hiding underneath waiting for people passing by. Three men and three women with guns jumped out. One man put a gun to my neck and I was very scared. At that time two tribes were fighting: Abgal and Habarrgidir. Their neighbourhoods were separated with a border to divide the two tribes. I was walking from one side of the border to the other. My house was in the Abgal area. I could tell he was Habarrgidir because of his accent and the side of the border he was on. The guy with the gun asked me where I was going. He then asked me if I was a news reporter who was working for the other side (Abgal). He asked me if I was going to tell other people what they were doing. I could tell he felt threatened. I said "I am Asharaf and it is not my business to tell other people what is happening." I said I was going to my house to get some things for my children. One of the women in the group said "Kill her far away so her blood

There is a word in our language, *abtriso*. It means "tell me your family back to the beginning."

does not touch us." He asked me to walk and held the gun at my back as I moved. I recited verses from the Koran as I did this. He then told me to turn around and face him. The gunman said, "The truth is what I need. Who are you and what is your tribe?"

In Somalia, it is important to learn your tribal ancestry. You have to know it all, so that if someone asks, you can recite it all the way back. There is a word in our language, *abtriso*. It means "tell me your family back to the beginning." Back home, children must learn their tribal lineage thirty generations back because they could get caught and killed if they say the wrong thing. That's how important it is. Thankfully, I knew both my tribal lineage and also my husband's. I knew that the militia was looking to kill people from my mother's tribe, Hawadle. I knew my husband's family ancestry very well so I recited my mother-in-law's tribal lineage instead of my mom's. My mother-in-law's was Habarrgidir, the same as the gunman. So I said I am Asharaf. My father is Asharaf and my mother is from Habarrgidir (which was not true). He asked me again which tribe and I said my mother's family was Sa'ad from Habarrgirdir, and then from Sa'ad, Reer Mohamad before that. He said, "What is your father's name? What is your mother's name?" I gave my mother-in-law's name instead of my real mother's. He said "Do you know a guy named so-and-so?" I said, "It is my mother's brother (really my mother-in-law's brother)." I was being tested. The gunman said "Okay, who else knows you in the neighbourhood?" I named a particular man and the gunman asked to speak with him. I said, "He has moved to another part of Mogadishu, but if you want, we can go and see him and he will tell you my father is Asharaf and my mother is Habarrgidir." He looked at me and said, "Get out of here and don't come back." I have tried to forget all this; I do not want to remember it.

This is how my house and all my possessions were taken from me. Later on, while fleeing yet again, I became separated from my children. I felt fear, anger and worry. In the beginning, I did not know if any of them was alive and then I heard my two daughters were safe in Italy. It took a long time to get the news, almost a year.

All the problems I went through in Somalia, now I do not think about them anymore. I have enough and I am with my family.

After becoming separated from my children, I became very sick with an ulcer – throwing up blood because of all the stress. At that time, I lived with other people who helped me. Eventually, I lived in Kenya for three months and then came to Canada. After arriving, I heard through the Somali community that my two daughters Sadia and Safia were in Vancouver. Eventually my son Omar and his family came to Canada too. The troubles in Somalia are still there today. I watch the Somali news on satellite TV. Just yesterday, there were seven Somali women who went shopping with their children and they all died in a bomb explosion.

My strength comes from my creator God and from my Muslim religion. It teaches us that if you are patient there will be relief and good will come. That is also how my father raised me. All the problems I went through in Somalia, now I do not think about them anymore. I have enough and I am with my family. Gratitude is also a big part of my faith. It is said that your blessings are countless. Even if you have little, there are always people who are doing even worse. Just to have fresh air to breath and to be in a safe place are blessings. People often complain about what they don't have, but instead it is important to be thankful to the creator. The Koran teaches that God promises those who are thankful will have an increase in blessings. It helps to be grateful. I say an Arabic phrase *Al-hamdulilah*, which means *thanks be to God*.

I am very devoted to my faith. I pray the five obligatory times a day that Muslims are asked to pray: before sunrise, around 12:30 or 1:00 p.m., late afternoon before sunset, after sunset, and before bed. But there are twelve other optional prayers in the day called *Suna* that I also pray, and I fast three days a month as well, which is optional. I live between hope and fear: the hope that I am a good Muslim and will go to paradise and the fear of God. I want to do what is right and keep a good conscience.

Here in Canada, there can be some division in the Somali community (as there can be in any community), but most of us do not think about tribal disagreements at all. We live in peace. The Somali community in Winnipeg calls me *Mama Raqiya* because everyone loves me and because I am respected. I have earned that name. Often when you live in Africa you have a whole extended family close by, but here in Canada, most of the Somalis do not have their mothers, so I am a mother to many of them. I go to the hospital and visit women who have had babies. But it's getting more difficult for me because I have problems with my legs.

Today, I am a student and a Canadian citizen. My daily life is simple. I go to English classes five mornings a week and at home, I read the Koran and pray and practice my English. I used to go to school on the weekends too, but I am getting too old, and it is so cold out in the winter. I do a lot of English homework because I need the repetition. I once said to my English teacher that I do not remember anything she teaches; when I leave class I have forgotten what I learned by the time I walk to the bus stop! The teacher was very encouraging. She said it is old age and not intelligence. But I must practice a lot. I also listen to the radio and watch TV. I rest. I have learned to be content.

> I live between hope and fear: the hope that I am a good Muslim and will go to paradise and the fear of God.

During our interview the translator, who is from the local Somali community, said this about Raqiya: "So many of us do not have our own mothers; Mama Raqiya is a mother to the Somali community here."

During the interview, there was tremendous sadness in Raqiya's eyes when she spoke about the hardest times in Somalia. It was clearly traumatic for her to remember the painful parts of her life that are now behind her. But she smiled brightly when talking about her Canadian citizenship. She is a very proud Canadian.

A special thank you to Omar Adan for his patience and generosity as translator.

EFREM

*In some ways, helping refugees is an added strain
when it interferes with things, but in other ways
it opens my heart and I see it as a strength.*

Since coming to Canada from Eritrea in 1989, I have sponsored at least fifty-eight new Canadians. At this time, we have about twenty-one others in the process of coming. My wife Nazareth was the first person I sponsored, but I'm not counting her in the total because she is my partner in all this, so really the first was her brother.

They were both refugees, having fled Eritrea for Athens. My wife had a concern leaving him behind in Athens when she knew she would be following me to Canada, so she asked if there was anything we could do and I was able to help him arrange his coming to Canada. In fact, before my wife even arrived in Winnipeg, I had sponsored my new brother-in-law. That was February 1990. Our siblings, cousins and cousins-in-law were among the next number of people we sponsored. After twenty-three years here, we still invite anyone we sponsor into our home, where they usually stay for three to six months. You may ask why my wife and I do this. Our parents taught us as children living in Eritrea to give generously without expecting something back. This is a guiding principle for us.

I was born in Eritrea in 1960. (At that time, Eritrea was not a country per se; it was seen as a region of Ethiopia. But in 1993, Eritrea gained its independence.) I was born in the capital city of Asmara where I lived until I completed my Grade 12 in 1978. I aspired to do post-secondary study. My parents raised me to believe education was number one. My dad would always tell my siblings and me, "I have no wealth to give you, but I'm going to make sure that you are educated. That will stay with you wherever you go."

I like hands-on jobs and thought engineering would fit my interests so I went to Addis Ababa University in Ethiopia's capital city to do my undergrad degree in engineering from 1979 to 1983. After I graduated, I worked for four years at a company called Ethiopian Water Construction. Being an Eritrean working in Ethiopia wasn't an ideal situation because of the political climate. For thirty years, there had been a civil war between the region of Eritrea and the rest of the country. I was looking for two things: a way to advance my education further and a way to relieve myself from the political situation by going to live somewhere else. Even though I was privileged to lead many projects in Ethiopia, I was always under suspicion and never treated fairly and equally because I was an Ethiopian of Eritrean origin. Being of Eritrean origin, I could be suspected of being in collaboration with the Eritrean People's Liberation Front (EPLF). Because the backbone of the liberation fighters were young high school and university students, the Ethiopian government could not distinguish who was what. All students were put under the same umbrella of suspicion.

Always being viewed with suspicion made me feel uncomfortable, and I had to go out of my way to prove I was not participating as a member of the liberation fighters. One time,

> My dad would always tell my siblings and me, "I have no wealth to give you, but I'm going to make sure that you are educated. That will stay with you wherever you go."

I was leading a project and the EPLF took some of our equipment. Immediately I was a suspect because of my Eritrean background and, therefore, thought to be collaborating with them. I was detained for three days, interrogated and abused a bit. I thought this is not the ideal place for me. I could not be certain of my future. Even though I was a project leader and one of those privileged, I was still under the cloud of suspicion and interrogation. Would a person of non-Eritrean background be interrogated if he were in my shoes? No. Those kinds of experiences started to resonate with me.

I applied for and got four scholarship offers to do my masters in engineering. Out of the four choices, the Ethiopian government allowed me to go to Delft Technical University in the Netherlands. My degree was in water resources, traditionally called hydraulic engineering. I finished my degree in 1989 and knew I didn't want to return to Ethiopia. At that time the economy was not great, and I knew I needed to go somewhere else to live, so I moved to France. I ended up working, but not in my field, just doing any job I could get because of the language and cultural barriers. First I worked as a cashier at the Southern Fried Chicken Restaurant, the French equivalent of Kentucky Fried Chicken. Then after six months, once my French had improved, I moved on to work for the City of Paris in an entry-level position in the Waste and Water department.

While I was living and supporting myself in Paris, I declared myself a refugee to the French government and asked for asylum. The process in France is similar to the one refugees have to go through in Canada. There was a hearing, and I had to justify myself and explain why I was in danger and what would happen if I returned. I demonstrated that I was unable to return to Ethiopia. I explained that if I went back there my life would be jeopardized; I could very likely be put in prison. At that time, there was documentation of how Eritreans were being persecuted by the Ethiopian government. People in circumstances similar to mine had returned and were in danger. This helped my case; it gave a clear signal to the French government that I was truly in need of asylum. It took from September '88 to February '89 for my application to be approved.

Around that time, my future wife, Nazareth, immigrated to Athens, Greece. We had met in

Eritrea after I graduated from university and she finished high school. We dated then, but we did not know what the future would be for either of us seeing I was leaving for Holland, so we did not make a long-term commitment. But after I left for Holland, we did stay in touch. Once she immigrated to Athens, I went to visit her and our relationship rekindled. We felt a good connection, so we made a commitment to each other. After that, I applied to immigrate to North America. I was fortunate to be accepted by both US and Canadian immigration, probably because I was young, had a post-graduate degree and was able to speak both English and French. I made my choice to come to Canada. No regrets. We were married in Athens in 1989, just before I moved to Canada. Nazareth followed me exactly eight months later.

Even though I came from France with the background of a refugee, I immigrated to Canada under the "skilled worker" classification because of my training as an engineer. My understanding at my interview in Paris was that it looked clear that my skills as an engineer were desirable in Canada, and I would work in the area I had trained for, but that was not to be the case. I was assigned to go to Montreal because I was perceived as bilingual, but I asked the immigration officers if I could go to Winnipeg because I had a cousin there. So I landed in Winnipeg on November 3, 1989. Initially, when I landed here I was so excited, but quickly realized I had to do something to support myself while I was pursuing my career as an engineer. I started working two to three hours a day as a waiter at the Winnipeg Squash Club and The Winnipeg Winter Club and on evenings and weekends, as a parking lot attendant. During this time I never felt frustrated or angry. I am a persevering person. I felt that I would work in my field eventually, but I had to come up with a strategy on how to make that happen. While doing these jobs, I took some computer courses and continued to aggressively pursue engineering-related jobs. Fortunately after four months, I learned that Manitoba Hydro was looking for an AutoCAD technician. I had learned this computer drafting skill in the Netherlands, so I was hired for a four-month term position. I was overqualified for the job – all that had been required was a one-year drafting course from Red River College – but I felt confident that it would lead me to a full-time engineering job.

I had been advised by a career counsellor at Canadian Manpower not to take the job, but it was my strategy to begin working there, demonstrate to the company what I could do, and then work my way up.

Looking back now, I can see it would have been easy to say, early on, that the system would not allow me to participate in my chosen field, that there were closed doors and a "big boys' club." But what is really behind an internationally educated immigrating engineer not getting the job he wants? Why does he have to drive a taxi instead? It has to do with comfort. When I am hiring an employee, my comfort zone lies with my confidence in the person I am interviewing, his or her level of experience in relation to the skills we are looking for, and the risk involved in hiring that person. If I compare graduates from the University of Manitoba to internationally educated engineers (IEE), hiring the person from the U of M is lower risk. That person is already part of the Canadian culture and educated here, while the IEEs are trained elsewhere and new to the culture. This creates a big unknown. If the employer knows the company would benefit more from hiring the immigrant, that's what will happen. But if they are not sure, they will make the less risky choice and hire the known. That could be interpreted as prejudice or discrimination, but it appears the safer choice for the employer.

When I was hired, there were a number of factors in my favour that helped me: being young and eager to work hard, having a tremendous curiosity and always challenging myself. One of my strengths is that when opportunity comes, I seize it, capitalize on it, and do not let go. I never want to limit myself. My good friend Doug Smart (an employment counsellor) calls me "very idealistic." He says I think everything is possible. That's true! Once I had the temporary position at Manitoba Hydro, I asked myself *why couldn't I work at Hydro permanently? Why not?* I believed that only I could convince my employer I would participate in a meaningful way once I knew their system. I ended up getting other temporary positions at Hydro afterward. I had a strong conviction about myself.

At the same time I was at Hydro, I was also working to get my Canadian Engineering licence. In order to practice as an engineer in Canada you need a licence from the

Association of Professional Engineers. As I worked as a technician at Manitoba Hydro, I wrote and finished these exams, but it took me almost two and a half years. This licence requirement was a big surprise to me. When I was considering immigrating from France, it was not communicated to me that I would need my Canadian licence to practise; I had no prior knowledge of that. At that time, we did not have the Internet, so information was limited. We could not get any information about these types of requirements from immigration officers abroad. Now immigrants are able to know the process; the information is out there. So after two and a half years, I was able to secure myself as a professional engineer with a full-time, permanent job at Manitoba Hydro.

During the time I was writing the exams for accreditation, I met Cass Booy a professor at the University of Manitoba who had also graduated from Delft Technical University. He suggested that while I was doing these exams, I could credit them towards a second master's degree in Hydraulics (water resource engineering) with a different focus of study. From there, I began progressing nicely at Hydro – from junior engineer to intermediate engineer,

and on to senior engineer. In 2009, I was appointed the Water Resource Engineering Department Head. I am one of the few, if not the only, immigrants of African origin to hold a management position there.

While I was pursuing my engineering career, my wife and I were also raising our family. (We have three teenager children.) And through all this, we continued to sponsor people mostly of Eritrean or Ethiopian background from many different places in Africa and Europe.

That first year I lived in Winnipeg was very intense, time-consuming and stressful: working multiple jobs, studying, getting settled and welcoming extended family. But at the same time, when I look back, my wife and I had the good fortune of having particular strengths that came from our early years in Africa. Both of us had grown up in large families: I grew up amongst ten siblings and my wife grew up with eight. There were certain hardships for us because of limited resources and having to share those with so many siblings. Our early years in Winnipeg were challenging, but relative to our upbringing, it was a comfortable hardship; food and shelter were not compromised; our basic needs were met. After that, our focus became our professions and gaining financial stability. If you've grown up with issues of being unsafe, nothing else seems too much to bear.

This is the attitude I take with me and try to pass on as we sponsor others to this country. Only about fifteen of the people we have sponsored have been family, people we had prior knowledge of. Some have been distant cousins who knew we were here and knew we would help. We would get a phone call from somewhere in Africa and the person would say, "I am the son of so and so" or "so and so referred me to you. Could you help me with sponsorship?" Some people could be related to us but we have not met them before. Others are friends of friends. We have even sponsored families from Kosovo and Afghanistan. My friend, Sister Aileen, has a sponsorship group that had run out of funds, and she came to me asking for help to sponsor people from other countries. They are still part of our lives today. In 2011, we sponsored the cousin of a friend of mine because she was stranded in Egypt looking to immigrate during the uprising.

> If you've grown up with issues of being unsafe, nothing else seems too much to bear.

There are certain criteria that must be followed in sponsoring immigrants. The criteria are quite clear on the federal and provincial governments' nominee websites. There are four categories for immigrants to fit into: family class, investor, skilled manpower, or refugee. So family can sponsor family, or if you have certain money to invest, you can come. "Skilled manpower" refers to immigrants who have skills that are needed in Canada – that is how I came.

In the refugee world, you can be sponsored three ways. There are churches that have an agreement with the federal government and undertake refugee sponsorship. There is also something called "the group of five" where five people can come together to sponsor someone. As well, the federal government has its own quota. It's preferred that there is a connection to others in Manitoba because the government wants people who will settle and stay in Manitoba. There is more likelihood of this if there is already extended family close by.

When we sponsor people and they live with us we provide them with all the basics they need – shelter, food, bus pass and clothing – without their paying anything. Our way of thinking is to have them save their money while living with us, which will contribute to their exit to independence later. Legally, we are responsible for them for the first year, but usually by six months they are ready to live on their own and have their own lives. The biggest challenge is helping them to find reasonable accommodations and jobs.

It is hard to find jobs that match their skill set. Each immigrant comes with different skills; some might have those that are transferrable to the Canadian market, but others may have skills they *think a*re useful, but really they do not have any relevance here in Canada. It is helpful to have a good learning capacity and at least some schooling. One of the most important things I can do for refugees is to help them to manage their frustrations. Most of the time I give them my personal example – I came here with a master's degree and a lot of education and ended up working as a waiter in the beginning. I tell them that if they have perseverance and persistence and are assertive they can get where they want to be, but to be prepared because there is a bumpy road ahead. We have a Yugoslavian friend who was a laborer in construction. Now he is one of the best floor refinishers, so I give him as an example too. He came with only limited education, but with a trade skill, and he lives very well. We have another friend who was an assistant nurse in her home country and is now a health care aide.

Canada is a land of opportunity. The opportunities come in different ways – they don't have to come just in Efrem's way. I have volunteered at and been on the board of the International Centre for ten years, so I have seen a lot of immigrants settle here. From this experience, I have a good sense as to where new people will end up. I have another friend who also had a master's degree, but who was older. He has found it very challenging, I think because of his age. Being older, it is often more difficult to adapt and accept the employment differences here. I would say the best luck is for those who are moderately educated – more so than highly educated – and for people with trades. Also it is better not to be too molded to the bureaucratic system before coming. I had a friend who worked for the United Nations in Cairo – a highly bureaucratic place – and it was hard for him to be flexible and adjust to change.

As sponsors we have to make sure that the immigrants feel there is always opportunity no matter what their age or circumstance.

I also have to be careful how I portray the opportunities; I do not want to give false hopes. More than seventy percent of immigrants do not come with skills because school is scarce in developing countries. They have to be realistic about job opportunities. My wife and I were lucky – we came to Canada knowing the English language, having transitioned to western countries from our time in Europe, and having a profession. It is much harder to come here alone or as a single parent with less family support, because most of those from developing countries are used to living communally, that is, having a lot of extended family support. In Canada, they are immediately asked by society to be more independent, private and individual. Lack of schooling and literacy also makes settling harder. But education is not just about learning letters and numbers; it opens your horizon for looking at things more broadly and making better decisions. If you have no education, you are limited to the things you knew growing up.

Some immigrants become frustrated when their expectations are not met, and then there's a danger that they will get extremely discouraged or make poor choices. They tend to blame the system, but it takes a lot of hard work and determination to succeed, and, of course, most who come here are very hard working. There was a federal study done which found that it takes most refugees or immigrants around ten years to catch up to the average Canadian socio-economic status level – but then they exceed it. I encourage most of them by saying that in five years, I would expect them to have a 1,000-square foot house. They are surprised if I suggest this, but sure enough, most do achieve that.

The commitment in sponsoring these people is truly a bit tiring. I need to balance my time spent on sponsorship with my time devoted to my marriage and the needs of my three children – especially now that they are teenagers and have lots of extra-curricular activities. My prime responsibility is to my immediate family. We lead a very structured life, and we make sacrifices. For example, when a refugee arrives, the first two days are challenging because their paperwork needs to be straightened out. Either my wife or I take a few of our vacation days to do this. One of our relatives characterizes us by saying "their hobby is to be like the UNHCR." She is right; but I do have other hobbies. I play soccer, read and bowl. I also volunteer on a number of boards. There are challenges though, and sometimes it creates strain in the family. Even though the refugee guests help out, our kids find it a strain to have extra people living in our home. I can't blame the children; like everyone else they want to have their parents to themselves. But over time, I have seen the kids come to embrace what we do. They have developed a desire to help. It is also especially difficult for my wife. There are many times she will say "As of today … enough! We need to live our own lives." But when a phone call comes, either from her side of the family or mine, we sit down and talk about it and say "Okay, this is the last one!" We've been saying that since 2005! The last one … the last one … the last one.

I am a very clear communicator and explain to our guests what is expected of them while they are living in our house. We set up the rules very quickly to develop a common understanding. My wife would say I am a straight shooter, and not overly sensitive.

Another big influence on me is that I am surrounded by people who spend their entire lives giving.

I would say I am pragmatic and have realistic expectations. My philosophy is to try consciously and diligently to help them so I do not have to feel guilty if later something is not working out for them. But sometimes we do worry. One thing that is particularly hard is if someone here is distressed for some reason. At times like that, I would say I just get more engaged. In fact, this intense engagement can even interfere with my work. Sometimes my boss will say "Efrem, you try to do too much. You only have twenty-four hours in the day." In some ways, helping refugees is an added strain when it interferes with things, but in other ways it opens my heart and I see it as a strength.

When I came to Canada, many people helped me to settle and get where I am today. Doug Smart (my friend and prior employment counsellor), my cousin and the people who sponsored me from the Osborne Village United Church supported me. I have that feeling that I have to give back. I have been honoured to get to know these people; they have shared their time, wisdom and resources with me. Another big influence on me is that I am surrounded by people who spend their entire lives giving. For example, Sister Aileen and Tom Denton, who both help a lot of refugees. I have worked with each of them over the years through their connections to International Centre and Hospitality House. I feel like my efforts are nothing compared to theirs.

But the biggest influences on me have been my father and the values I grew up with. I was the fourth of ten children; I shared everything with my siblings. I was very close with my parents growing up, but especially with my dad. My father was a very giving person. If he saw someone in need wandering around our town, he would invite that person to come and have lunch. My siblings used to say that I looked like him, thought like him and even spoke like him. My mom and dad passed away in 2006, but they had lived in Winnipeg for five years before that. I sponsored them and they brought two of my sisters with them. It was a dream come true to once again live in the same city as they did. Because of the way we had grown up – the turmoil of our native country and being separated many times – I had not spent time as an adult talking to my mom and dad. I knew them only as they were when I was a child. So

I strongly encouraged them to come and live with us in Canada. I told them that I wanted to spend time and get to know them better. While they lived in Winnipeg, every summer I would take two-weeks vacation with my wife and children and then I would go ten days

on the road somewhere alone, only with my mom and dad. I felt the best time to learn from them and to listen to them would be on these road trips. I asked a lot of questions and learned about our family history. That period of time and connection with my parents was a privilege.

Before I left Eritrea for the Netherlands in 1987, my father gave me a gold ring. I still wear it today, next to my wedding ring. On it is an engraving of a flower and a stem of wheat in a circle, because my dad's background was farming and it was very important to him. It was clear to my dad that I would not be back. He told me he was giving me the ring to remind me to always look back to where I had grown up. When I look at this ring I think of family.

> Before I left Eritrea for the Netherlands in 1987, my father gave me a gold ring. I still wear it today, next to my wedding ring.

I am lucky – but maybe the better word is blessed. My wife and I are both close with our families. We work well together; we have the good fortune to share the same values. Nazareth is patient, caring, supportive, and a great wife and mother.

Once you live in Manitoba, you know what this place can offer and the value of living here, but if we look at Manitoba from the outside, we see it is in the middle of nowhere, far from everything and with a long, cold winter. Pictured like this, this province does not sound attractive. But when we live here, we see the pace of living, and the decency and then we can say with gladness, *this is home.* Manitoba has a strong presence of private sponsorship. I think it comes from a deep-rooted history of immigration support starting after WWII when the province provided a home, early on, to eastern European immigrants. One of the founders of what is now called the International Centre (a well-established service provider for immigrants) was a nun. Many people and organizations have spent long hours lobbing the governments on behalf of immigrants. Many of the churches helping with sponsorship in Manitoba, exist in other provinces too: Mennonite, Lutheran, Catholic, and Presbyterian. These churches are everywhere, but those in other provinces do not seem to have the experience of the ones in Manitoba.

I started to see Canada as home very shortly after arriving. I have always had the strength of learning easily. But throughout my life, I was looking for a place to settle where nothing would be in my way and I did not fear for my life, a place where, in a sense, I would feel secure to really *live*. (That can so easily be taken for granted.) I never felt secure until I arrived in Winnipeg. Living in Ethiopia, I thought my life deserved better. Canada gave me that opportunity. I thought if Canada can provide me with security to live without fear every day, to live the way I want, then this is home. Why would I want to live anywhere else?

Efrem has been tremendously successful, but as a new Canadian especially so, having per-severed to break through the often frustrating employment ceiling many immigrants experi-ence. But he spoke of his success in a humble and matter-of-fact way.

Efrem says he is a big fan of Joan Lunden who years ago moved from a small US town to New York to host the Good Morning America TV show. He appreciates her writ-ing on family. She says there are two kinds of family: family by kin and family by choice. Although Efrem has a large number of

extended family members he has sponsored over the years, it is his family by choice he is especially grateful for. Efrem values these people he's met in Winnipeg (among them Doug Smart, Tom Denton, Denis Fisher and Donna Beljanic) who have come to be like family to him.

NOMA

*And when does a person stop being a newcomer
and become Canadian?
When can we call this country home?*

I was born in Zimbabwe, but I lived for twenty years in the United States before I came to Canada in 2005 at the age of twenty-four. And yet, I came here because I felt I had to leave the US. Did I come to Canada as an immigrant, or as a refugee? Technically, I came as an immigrant, but I do think of myself as a refugee of sorts, because I felt I was fleeing.

Growing up, I felt like an all-American girl. But when I had to leave that country, I was reminded that I had come from somewhere else.

Rhodesia gained independence from British colonial rule and changed its name to Zimbabwe in 1980, just before I was born in 1981. But I have no real memories of Zimbabwe, just of people there. My father left in 1985 and my mother, brother and I followed one year later in 1986. I have never been back, but I've always dreamed of returning one day. My father felt it was unsafe for us to stay in Zimbabwe after the country's political independence. There had been two banned political parties of the people fighting for independence in the '70s. My parents had aligned themselves with the Zimbabwe African People's Union (ZAPU) founded and led by my mother's uncle Joshua Nkomo. The other party was Robert Mugabe's Zimbabwe African National Union (ZANU). After independence Robert Mugabe was made president. My great-uncle, although opposed to Mugabe, still served as Vice President of Zimbabwe in Mugabe's government in the 1990s. Nkomo was declared a national hero and affectionately named *Father Zimbabwe*.

After independence there was tension between the two parties. My father was seen as being biased against Mugabe's government due to his party affiliations. I know my father was feeling unsafe but did not want to leave his country. Then violence escalated. I found out many years later that some family members had disappeared too. This all made my father realize it was time to leave.

While I was growing up, my parents did not talk much about Zimbabwe. There were a lot of things unsaid. My mother would speak mostly about our friends and family. I know a little more about my mom's family background, but that's because there are books written about her family. My father has said very little. My family history is something I'm still trying to learn about.

Fortunately, my father was educated, so he applied to do his masters in 1986 at the Iliff School of Theology in Denver and was accepted. My younger brother Tha was just a baby when we came and my youngest brother Khanya was born in the US. My immediate family was able to come to the United States under my father's student visa. We lived in the university's family residences when we first arrived. There were many international students there with a wide variety of customs and traditions. I was young and remember very little of that transitional time in our lives. I have a lot of early memories of people and of playing with other kids. I do not even remember learning English. In my mind, I just always knew it. I remember this as a happy time. But now that I am older, I see that there were a lot of adjustments for my parents, such as the cultural differences and isolation from family members far away. The move put a great strain on my parents.

Much later, when I was a young adult, my uncle helped me to understand how difficult leaving would have been for my parents. He told me about his generation having fought for their country's independence and then the painful feelings of not even being able to live in Zimbabwe. I realized this must be how my parents felt. As a child, I did not even know they had been a part of the freedom movement. I remember when my dad's brother died, I saw my father cry for the first time. He could not even go to the funeral. As a child I could not understand this. Hearing all this from my uncle was a turning point for me. My eyes were opened. It helped me to understand everything my parents had given up to give me this life, this opportunity in North America.

After a few years, we moved to the University Park area in Denver. I loved this neighbourhood. We lived on the corner of Iliff and University. Because of the close proximity of our neighbourhood to the university, we got to know people from different countries who were affiliated with the school. Although it was generally a homogeneous, white neighbourhood, our little block of houses, including a ten-unit apartment complex, was diverse. We kind of banded together. There was Kim – who I called Uncle Kim. He was from Korea, and had two children, Johan and Melissa. Kim would discipline us just as easily as our own parents. Charmaine, my best friend at the time, was from the Philippines. Another good friend was Deanne. She was one of the few white Americans who lived on our block. Her family was not connected with the university, but we brought her into the fold. We all watched out for each other. And we'd regularly eat dinner at each other's homes. Deanne and I became mother hens to all the younger kids on the block. We even started a free neighbourhood summer camp when we were twelve or thirteen. We were organized – we had a definite schedule and activities. We'd walk the kids to the elementary school, play games and have picnics. I remember we even had a mini Olympics on a jungle gym. All the parents knew about our "camp," and everyone participated. For two weeks, we were free babysitters. That was a time when people still

> My eyes were opened. It helped me to understand everything my parents had given up to give me this life, this opportunity in North America.

felt safe about their communities and parents were comfortable letting their children have more freedom. I just loved that way of living. When I remember that place and time, I think of the phrase "it takes a village to raise a child." That was our neighbourhood and everybody embodied that belief.

Looking back now, I see there were two Nomas inside of me then and sometimes they were at odds with each other. When I was at home or with the African communities I was Zimbabwean and felt comfortable with that to a certain extent. We spoke our native language, Sindebele, at home, and my mom gave us language lessons for an hour a day for a long time. We are Ndebele heritage (an off-shoot of Zulu).

> Looking back now, I see there were two Nomas inside of me then and sometimes they were at odds with each other.

But then there was the Noma who went to school and was the all-American girl. But there were limitations there. My parents were strict. When I tried to talk back to them like some of my American-born friends did to their own parents, that did not fly, not AT ALL.

And then there was the first day of school each year, and any day a substitute teacher came. Those were the days the teachers would have to pronounce my full name – Nomaqhawe. They could never do it. By third grade, I had perfected how to handle the situation. I would be sure to sit in the front, especially if we had a substitute and did not have assigned seating. I wanted to follow where the teacher was on the class list. I would think *okay, I'm next. I come after Sarah Rector.* Sure enough, as the teacher struggled to say my name, "Noma-kawee, Nomaco-wee," I'd shout, "It's Noma!" Being different and from somewhere else has become "cool" only recently. It was not cool then. Kids can be cruel. Kids used to ask where I was from and I'd say Zimbabwe, Africa. At the time the only thing kids could relate to Africa was the Eddie Murphy movie *Coming to America.* Kids would ask me if I was an African princess and I can remember being a bit of a liar and saying, "Oh ya, totally." They would ask if I played with elephants and lions. But then, the flip side was having kids say I was an African bootie scratcher or calling, "Hey Kunta Kinte" because the TV series *Roots* was popular then. So my identity depended on where I was. I used to say to myself, *I am American, I am American, I am American*. I think my parents wanted that for us too – to fit in. But I also think they feared completely letting go and saying to us, "Okay, just be American" because they were proud of where we had come from.

When I was in high school, I had a few opportunities to travel outside the US. The most important one was a chance to travel to Australia as a United Nations youth ambassador. But my parents said I could not go; the government would not allow it. Shortly after our arrival in the US, my dad had taken a brief trip back to Zimbabwe. After his return to America, I was told our Zimbabwean passports had been taken, for our safety. I never really talked to my parents about this so I have never understood why that happened. At first I did not know that my parents had started the process of seeking political asylum in the US, so they would not have to face returning to Zimbabwe permanently. Then, one day during that time, I was looking for a document on my parents' computer and I found a letter to the US government. That's how I learned they were seeking asylum and that family members back in Zimbabwe had disappeared. I think my parents were trying to protect us by not talking

about our immigration issues. Not being able to go on school trips was a reminder that I was not from the United States. I was not a citizen; I was a visitor.

In 2000, a deportation letter came addressed to my parents. It was my first semester of university at Colorado State in Fort Collins about an hour away. My parents phoned and told me I needed to come to Denver for an immigration meeting. My parents didn't really say much – because that was my parents' way. I had become frustrated not having American citizenship. I did not understand why I couldn't get it, and that had become a cause of disagreement between my parents and me. I hoped that since I was eighteen, maybe during the meeting I would be given my own status and my own citizenship. So I went down to Denver for the day. We all drove to the meeting in one car, and on the way my father said, "So the government is deciding whether or not we can stay in the US." The hysteria hit. I remember trying to stay calm, because in my family you don't cry. My parents said, "It's okay if we have to leave; we'll probably go to England. We've got cousins there." When I think now about their response to the circumstances, I think my

dad could say that, because he had lost the only place he had ever really loved – his home country of Zimbabwe. So he could live anywhere. But my brothers and I started crying, because we did not want to go. By the time we arrived at the immigration office, we were already traumatized.

I remember going into the immigration office. The guy who was to interview us was Hispanic, with glasses, and he had Dave Matthews's music playing in the background. He treated us like a file number. He did not make eye contact, and I could see my parents were being submissive – even my dad. It was off-putting. I remember studying the immigration officer and thinking, *You might be from here. Your family might have been in the US for generations, I don't really know. But where did your family originate? When did they arrive? At some point your family would have migrated from somewhere else. I like Dave Matthews too. I just went to his concert. Come on! I'm just as much a citizen as you are.* And I didn't understand what was going on in the meeting because I didn't have enough information. I was holding onto my chair to keep myself from crying; not just because we might possibly have to move, but also because of the way he was treating us. I felt like he was implying that we were parasites and we did not belong there.

We left that day and nothing more was said by my parents. I returned to school and we waited. Then in the spring of 2002, my parents surprised me by saying our family would be moving very quickly to Canada. It was not even the end of the semester, but they told me I had to wind things up at school and look into transferring universities. They said we would be going to Manitoba and there were good universities there. At that time, Canada had opened its borders to Zimbabwean refugees. Those holding a Zimbabwean passport, even if they were already living elsewhere, would be accepted in Canada. Somehow, our passports had been returned to us. My mother had given me mine. For months, my parents had been carefully making a plan. They had appealed deportation letters in the past, but now they knew their situation could no longer be stayed. If they did not leave voluntarily the American government could prohibit re-entry. They were trying to gauge what the decision of their case would be, so that if they were deported, they'd already have a plan. My parent's Brethren in Christ Church community had developed a connection with the strong Mennonite community in Manitoba, so they felt there was a base of support and Manitoba would be the best choice.

I came to see them right away. While I was there, I told my mother I didn't think I was going to go with them. I was just not getting that sense from God; I was not hearing that voice internally. She cried and cried. I'd wake up at 2:00 in the morning and hear her crying. I was not ready to move, plain and simple. I would have lost a whole year at university and would have had to start all over again. Examining the citizenship of students did not become a priority for the government until after 9/11, a few months later in 2001. I felt that as long as I was in school and living at another address, I was safe. The system was fragmented and the government would not know where I was. I decided I was going back to school and I would see what happened. So I said goodbye and drove back to my apartment. I prayed about my decision,

Then in the spring of 2002, my parents surprised me by saying our family would be moving very quickly to Canada.

and when I woke up the next day, I did not start packing. Instead I picked up my book bag and went to class.

My parents packed whatever they could fit into their two cars and left quickly with my brothers. They didn't even have a place to live. My dad said they were petrified as they approached the Canadian border, because of how they had been treated by US immigration. The Canadian customs officers just asked my father a few questions and did not give him a hard time.

Time passed, and I stayed in Colorado until just after I graduated in 2005. Afterwards, I had plans to go to graduate school in Italy. I had an aunt who had a close friend there and I could live with her and her family. My parents had agreed to pay for my graduate school. They knew I was strong-minded and I was planning to go, but one day, as my application was due, they said "no". They wanted me to move to Canada and get my citizenship so I could finally settle my whole immigration situation. They asked me to think about whether I wanted to deal with this for the rest of my life. In Italy, it is a ten-year commitment to apply for citizenship. I thought about it and knew they were right. Although I had never received a deportation letter, I did not want to have problems later. I wanted citizenship so I could have my freedom.

At the time, my boyfriend brought up the subject of marriage. He asked me if it was something I wanted, not just so I could stay in the country, but because he wanted to be with me. I knew he wanted to settle in his hometown. I loved him and Colorado, but I knew that if I married him, it would be to stay in his town, and I was not ready for that kind of commitment. I had crossed this path once before with another boyfriend in 2002. I was just twenty-one then. He had asked me the same question. I remember feeling really desperate because I did not want to leave the US, but in my soul I did not feel that getting married was the right decision.

Leaving the United States was bittersweet. I was leaving on my own terms, which is very different from being asked to leave, but I also knew I didn't have a choice in staying. I had

> My dad said they were petrified as they approached the Canadian border, because of how they had been treated by US immigration.

already stayed for an extra three years. But I did receive my university degree and I had the opportunity to say goodbye to my friends. There was a sort of closure; unlike for my brothers who had to leave quickly. There is a quotation by Barbara Law that is appropriate: "An immigrant leaves his homeland for greener grass. A refugee leaves his homeland because the grass is burning under his feet." Being forced to flee is traumatizing; it creates emotional baggage. On the other hand, I had had time to process the trauma of knowing one day I would have to leave. There was a side of me that wanted to travel and see new places. I had planned to be leaving for graduate school anyway; I was just leaving for a different reason and a different place instead.

I am a bit of a planner and I love to research things on the Internet. So I had already googled Winnipeg. I thought St. Boniface sounded interesting. I felt optimistic because I love adventure and also because I felt I would be leaving my immigration battles behind. I had planned to move in August and enroll at the University of Winnipeg. Then my permanent resident status, which my parents and I had applied for, was delayed so I did not arrive in Manitoba until October. A few weeks before coming, my parents explained that if I was not going to university, then they saw no sense in paying for me to rent an apartment in Winnipeg. Suddenly I was faced with having to live with them. They lived in the small town of Steinbach, sixty-five kilometres away.

I was twenty-five years old; I lasted two months in Steinbach. It was too quiet and conservative for me. Also, I realized I could not live with my parents. I had already been living independently for four years. It was a stressful time. The first week was okay; it snowed, I looked around, I went to church. One day, my mom was running errands, so I went with her. I remember sitting in the car waiting for her while she was at the drugstore. A woman knocked on my car window. I opened the door and she asked me if I was Noma. I thought *Oh my God! Seriously? I guess there aren't many black women in Steinbach.* She recognized the car and knew my parents from church. She was

> Being forced to flee is traumatizing; it creates emotional baggage. On the other hand, I had had time to process the trauma of knowing one day I would have to leave.

married to a white Zimbabwean, Darryl, the man who had helped my parents settle.

A lot of people came by our house my first week. But then by the second week the honeymoon had worn off. I was bored; I was not attending university, I had no job and knew no one. A man at church who was well connected offered to help me look for a job when I was ready. I said, "What are you doing Tuesday? Do you want to go for coffee?" Eventually, I found a job as a legal assistant in Winnipeg, and moved there shortly after. Although it was a difficult time and I knew no one, I had the power of choice because I lived in North America. I was not living restricted in a refugee camp. I did not have to feel stuck.

When I first came to Canada I was angry, not at Canada or a person but at my situation. Initially my reaction was *Give me my citizenship already. I'm just squatting here until I get it and then I'm outta here!* I thought Canada owed it to me somehow. But then I started thinking, *Why does Canada owe me anything?* Now that I have been living here a while, my attitude has changed. I no longer want to use the country like a prostitute. I have a tremendous respect for Canada. The longer I live here, the more things I find to love about this country. Canada is not as individualistic as the US; people here seem to take care of each other more.

My immigration experiences in the US and now Canada have made me want to work with newcomers. I want to give a voice to my experience and help others navigate theirs. At Immigrant Refugee Community Organization of Manitoba (IRCOM) where I volunteer now, we grapple with "what is a newcomer." How do we define that? And when does a person stop being a newcomer and become Canadian? When can we call this country home? Newcomers may wonder whether by letting go of the newcomer title they are letting go of where they came from. Perhaps those in the community, long-time Canadians, have a hard time relinquishing the use of the word also, because of what it may be tied to. Because I look and sound North American, I have

> Although it was a difficult time and I knew no one, I had the power of choice because I lived in North America. I was not living restricted in a refugee camp. I did not have to feel stuck.

fewer boundaries and people seem comfortable around me. For this reason, I've heard some established Canadians and Americans voice their private thoughts on immigrants; not realizing I am one too. It always amazes me what people will say. The views are not always nice. There is a feeling of entitlement by long-time residents, but also a lack of understanding.

At the University of Colorado, I joined the African Students' Union. One guy there told me I was not even African. Some African-Americans had already told me something similar, but that was the first time an African told me that I did not belong. My friends, both black and white, have said to me, "You seem white. You're white underneath with brown on top." But I'm not; I'm not white! Initially when I arrived in Winnipeg and was surrounded by so many people from different countries and no one was saying to me you don't act black, you don't sound black, I thought *Ah! This is it! Canada is progressive.* But now, having lived here a little longer, I am constantly reminded that I am American, not Canadian. If you ask me where I am most comfortable,

my honest answer right now is I don't know. As I have grown up, I see there are things about the Zimbabwean culture I do not agree with, such as women serving men and men eating before women. The argument is "But as a good Zimbabwean woman you should…" Well I guess I am not a good Zimbabwean woman! It just doesn't fit for me. I see that I'm still trying to figure out where I belong.

As I've gotten older, I've come to see my multicultural identity not as opposing sides of myself as I did as a child, but as a hybrid identity. I am Zimbabwean by heritage, with an American childhood and since March 2011 a full Canadian with citizenship. I am content with my identity for now. I understand who I am at this moment. It's like I have a foot in each culture, and yet I can step back and observe.

I call Colorado my heart home and Zimbabwe my soul home. I call the us my heart home because even with everything that has happened, I've had so much opportunity there. It's where I grew up and I want to give thanks to the us. I look at all the political problems in Zimbabwe and wonder what my life would have been like if my

> If you ask me where I am most comfortable, my honest answer right now is I don't know.

family had never left. Even the people who were well off there are struggling now. When I was younger, I wrote a poem titled *Bury me in Africa*. Even though I have not returned, I feel such a connection to Zimbabwe, because of the people I know and the traditions my parents have raised me in. That is why I call Zimbabwe my soul home.

Now that I can travel freely, I hope to visit Zimbabwe soon. I am interested in history and I want to see where it began for me. I want to see my elderly family there. I've heard about a great uncle in a hut somewhere who knows our genealogy and family tree. I want that for myself, that feeling of being rooted in history. Maybe that's because I haven't yet had a place to feel fully rooted. But then I worry – what if the idea of Zimbabwe being my soul home is just a fantasy. When I return, how will I feel? I'm kind of scared. I have a Zimbabwean friend who grew up in a rural area. He said now that he lives in the city and travels back to the countryside to visit, he doesn't quite fit in there anymore. Going to Zimbabwe could complete me, but I could also become heartbroken. I

> But then I worry – what if the idea of Zimbabwe being my soul home is just a fantasy. When I return, how will I feel?

panic over not knowing the answer to my latest question of identity. But I do have a feeling that when I go to Zimbabwe, it will be full circle for me. I will be looking for a sense of home and identity. For now, a number of things are open ended. This is all part of my journey and it will make sense in time.

Noma says she realized that living a life of opportunity meant, for her, more of a responsibility to help others, particularly those in Africa. She says this comes from her belief that much should be asked of those who have much. Noma and a group of friends founded the charitable organization Raindrops in 2010, which works for health and educational initiatives. Their first initiative was to send a shipment of medical supplies and soccer equipment to Zimbabwe. They are currently working on a pilot project with the UNHCR preparing to distribute dignity kits to women in the Botswana refugee camp of Dukwi. These kits contain underwear and a few basic hygiene items. Noma told me that underwear is a

need that can be overlooked because it is
simple and practical, yet it is something that
isn't available to everyone.

Noma plays guitar and is a member of
the band Guerillas of Soul. She wants to use
music to generate social change. She says
music is for her "a way to story tell when
the literal tale is too complex or painful
to recount."

AKIM

I remember being outside the day after the Militia raid and almost all of my playmates were gone. It was utter destruction. This was the end of life in the village as we had known it.

My first experience of violence happened around 1960 when I was an innocent boy of about four. I was living in Muyuka, my mother's small village in southern Sudan. My friends and I were playing outside my family's hut when I suddenly saw men in long white robes running into our village. I had never seen visitors like this before.

Our African village was deep in the bush, with a footpath leading to a circle of mud-and-brick, thatched-roof huts. All of a sudden, these men came rushing in with guns and started attacking our village. They were government militia from Khartoum, the capital city of Arab-dominated northern Sudan. I was one of the lucky ones who fled. I ran to my grandfather's coffee plantation just 100 metres from the centre of the village. I hid there, staying low, but I could see and hear the attack. I saw children and women being tied up and taken away – to be sold as slaves, I now know. Some people were forced into huts, the doors jammed and the huts set on fire. There was chaos and screaming everywhere. It was terrifying. Most of the older adults were left alone, because they were of no use to the soldiers. I vividly remember watching the whole horrifying scene around me. I stayed there hidden for two or three hours until everything was all quiet again.

I was too young to know who the militia were or what they were doing. My mother had not yet told me about the politics of Sudan at that time. I did not know about the deep divide between the Arab-dominated North, based in Khartoum, and the tribal farmers and herders of the South. That invasion was a total surprise to me. When I finally returned to my home I found both my mom and my younger brother alive. When they heard the militia coming, they had run from the village. Just like me, they had hidden and were not found. Later thinking back, I would realize how lucky I was that we had all survived. I remember being outside the

I did not know about the deep divide between the Arab-dominated North, based in Khartoum, and the tribal farmers and herders of the South.

day after the militia raid and almost all of my playmates were gone. It was utter destruction. This was the end of life in the village as we had known it, because few wanted to chance staying there in case there was another attack.

My father was living, at that time, in Uganda outside Kampala, where he was a primary school teacher. News of the attack had reached him across the border in Uganda, about 330 miles away. Several days later, he arrived. I had not known anything about him until he showed up that day. My mother told us, "This is your dad. He has come to take us away from southern Sudan because the war is coming." We left on bicycles carrying whatever we could. I have a vivid memory of many, many families travelling the route to Uganda together: thousands of people moving in a line, carrying their possession and their children, hoping for safety in the neighbouring country. My mother's parents stayed behind with a small community of older villagers who also did not want to leave. My grandfather could not abandon his village. He was an industrious man; a carpenter and a farmer who had a farm full of corn, millet, sorghum and many fruits and vegetables. Even without us, they would continue on in Muyuka.

Initially, it was difficult living together in Uganda, because my father was somebody I had never even met before. I had to learn to know him. I was shy at first, and I noticed the unease in the relationship between him and my mother, because they had been separated for so many years. Eventually we lived a regular life together, with a strong emphasis on schooling. My parents, especially my dad, wanted to make sure I got an education. I was able to attend the school where he taught, in a town named Masindi, outside Kampala. In Sudan, there was no chance for education, but in Uganda I progressed from one class to the next throughout my childhood, until I went to university.

In 1972, when I was about thirteen, the Addis Ababa agreement was signed between the South and North of Sudan. So my parents, like many other south Sudanese, decided to return. But with the educational opportunities being better in Uganda, I stayed on and boarded at the school I was attending; Kiira College outside the town of Jinja. During the school holidays, I went to be with my aunt

in the town of Mukono outside Kampala. A Christian non-government organization paid for my education. In Uganda, university is free, so after high school, I attended Makerere University in Kampala. I studied economics and statistics.

In 1979, during my second year of university, my life was changed again because of conflict. Tanzania was angry at Uganda for a prior attack so it retaliated together with the insurgents who were unhappy with the government of then Ugandan leader Idi Amin. There was a huge exodus of people leaving the city. Trucks full of Ugandan refugees were heading eastward to Kenya, thousands and thousands of people fleeing in anticipation of the rebels entering Kampala. I had packed a few possessions and my papers in a travel bag, and I was in the main part of town trying to find transportation. I was planning to go north towards a town in Uganda called Arua. It just so happened that a truck loaded down with people stopped close to me, and it was driven by the father of one of my students. (At the time, besides going to university I was teaching high school part time, while university was on holidays.) One of my students, a Somali girl of about fifteen, approached me and said, "Teacher where are you going? Why don't you come with us; we are going to Nairobi. There is going to be a war in Kampala any day now. It is not going to be safe." I said okay and got right on that truck for Nairobi. I was unbelievably lucky; I will never forget that girl. A short time later Kampala fell.

When our truck approached the Kenya-Uganda border, there were crowds of people and much disorganization. But we were able to cross into Kenya easily. The next day, we reached the city of Nairobi. I got off that truck covered in dust, and a stranger came out of nowhere and offered to take me to his house to clean up. That is the African way – to see someone in need and to help, regardless of whether the person is a stranger. I wish I had kept in touch with these people who helped me out of the kindness of their hearts because I feel I owe them something.

That is the African way – to see someone in need and to help, regardless of whether the person is a stranger.

Once in Nairobi, I managed to get a plane ticket from the Sudanese embassy back to Sudan, which was made easier by the fact that there was a general evacuation of the Sudanese refugees now living in Kenya who had fled from Uganda when the fighting began. I returned to Juba, Sudan where my parents lived. They had been terrified because they didn't know if I had survived in Uganda. I was anxious to finish my university degree, but there was no infrastructure for universities in Sudan. So every day I went to government offices looking for funding to study overseas. I applied to many universities, including the University of Ottawa. The first to accept me was the University of Ulster in Northern Ireland. I managed to get funding to go there from the minister of education in the South Sudanese Regional Government.

Ireland is a beautiful country, and I found the people there to be very nice. Even though I had studied English in school my whole life, an Irish accent was totally different for me, and I could not understand it at first. But I managed to catch on quickly. I spent three years there studying mathematics and operational research. I graduated in the summer of 1982 and returned to Sudan later that year.

My friends were waiting for me back home. They said, "Akim we have a big job here to do. There are lots of problems in south Sudan." The soldiers of the Arab dominated North were again attacking villages and the country was regressing. Children were very hungry and there was a lot of poverty. So before I could even settle down, I actively found people focused on local politics and joined them. In those days, my mom wondered why I was out all the time. She thought I had a girlfriend, but actually I was busy with political meetings.

A brief history of the country of Sudan shows that 700 years ago, a large number of Arabs migrated south from Egypt to central Sudan. They did not come to be a part of the country; they came to occupy it and make it their own territory. Their mandate was to dominate the economy and politics and control the Nile Valley land and vast resources in Sudan. As well they wanted to enslave all African tribes there. Everyone was affected by this. The British and the Egyptians also ruled for a period of time in the 1800s. In 1956, once the British left, the local Sudanese began to understand politics and to challenge the northern government's rulings. War broke out and continued until 1972 when a peace agreement was reached in Addis Ababa.

There was a period of relative peace between 1972 and 1982.

But the goals and priorities of the northern Sudanese continued to be different from those of the southern Sudanese. So when I returned in 1982, underground cells opposed to the northern government were forming. People were asking themselves what should be done. We advocated a continued campaign through publications. Our purpose was to educate the ordinary southern Sudanese about what was seriously wrong in south Sudan and to get support for our ideas. These problems focused on the silent suffering of southerners due to the controlling tactics of the North. The South was very deliberately exploited for their resources. We wanted roads, healthcare and education. South Sudan is the size of England and France combined, but had only three miles of paved roads. Starvation was commonplace and an alarming number of women were dying during childbirth. It was a tragedy. We wanted to inform others of these conditions by handing out documents to people on the streets and writing letters to prominent people. Our cell wrote a secret document we called the Manifesto for the Liberation of South Sudan. In that document, we advocated the liberation of the South by all means available. I was excited to work to affect change, but there was frustration that the ruling North would not take our actions seriously. They called the southerners *Abid*, Arabic for slaves. People were looking for every means possible to create change, but it seems to me that the majority of the south Sudanese knew there was no way to wrestle their region out of the control of the Arab-dominated North without violence. There were a lot of student riots and many students were killed in the streets. There were several demonstrations against the government and against then President Gaafar Nimeiry. Contributing to this uprising was President Nimeiry's decree to make Sudan an Islamic state. This became a prelude of what was to happen to me.

In 1983, the government got hold of one of the documents my friends and I had been circulating. My name had appeared on them because I was one of the people writing and distributing this educational material, so they began searching for me. On February 2, I was arrested, along with a number of my friends, and taken to prison. We were severely and repeatedly tortured in the interrogation quarters. I lost consciousness many times from electric shocks and beatings. I had bruises all over my body and, at one point, had a gun held to my head with threats of being killed. They wanted us to reveal further information and the names of people who were associated with us. This routine went on for sixty days. The first few weeks I said, "This is it, let it be done (death)," but I was young and the desire to live came back – I just did not want to give up. Still, it was very tough. They used to come for us at any time in the night. For years afterward I had nightmares; I would wake up and fear being captured, not knowing where I was.

Prison life was extremely hard. We were ten people to a cell and the washroom was a bucket in the corner. It was smelly, just terrible. We slept on mattresses on the floor. In a way, though, we considered ourselves lucky because we young rebels were classified as political prisoners. They mixed us together with others who were actively against the government – prominent south Sudanese politicians, for example, who were known outside their communities and by journalists. They treated these people with some respect because they had to. So we had certain privileges that the other prisoners did not. Our families could bring us bed sheets for our mattresses and food each day. My mother cried every day when she came. She would always say to me, "Why didn't you wait until I was gone from this earth to get involved in these things?" I would tell her, "Mom I'm already in here; you've got to live with it."

My colleagues and I found we could correspond with the outside world. We managed to sneak letters out by putting them in the thermos flasks our families brought tea in. We would unscrew the bottom and place the letters in the inner walls. If our friends outside wanted to send us a message, they would put a tiny letter folded in a piece of cornmeal bread. They used to give us instructions, or tell us about the outside world.

For all the other prisoners, jail was a nightmare. There was very little food and their conditions were even worse than ours. Those who were physically fit were made to work hard labour on farms. There were children in this prison, captured off the streets for stealing a little food. Another section of the

> For years afterward I had nightmares; I would wake up and fear being captured, not knowing where I was.

prison was for the mentally unstable people who had been living in the streets. They were left in their excrement, chained to the ground and bleeding because they struggled to get free. Their hunger, their smell, and the conditions they lived in were appalling.

It was our bed sheets that saved us. One thing we had decided was that we were not going to wait for the final trial, but we were going to try to escape. Then on April 2, 1983, there was a very powerful storm; it destroyed buildings in Juba and knocked out the power in the prison just before they locked the doors for the night. It was completely dark inside and out. I told my friends, "The doors are open; there are no lights. This may be our one chance to escape." We grabbed our bed sheets and some clothes and headed straight to the eighteen-foot wall surrounding the prison. All the guards who usually sat on top of that wall had come down to take shelter because the storm was so powerful. There were five of us together that night. The two tallest guys got on the wall and pulled the rest of us over. We did not have a lot of physical strength, but the adrenaline was there. It was a moment we just had to seize. We became injured and bruised from our efforts, but we were free. We escaped out of the prison and into the banana plantations. We disappeared out there, changed our clothes and started off. Amazingly, as soon as we started walking the storm stopped. We were told that when the guards went to lock the doors and didn't find us, the alarm was sounded and the hunt for us began.

> I told my friends, "The doors are open; there are no lights. This may be our one chance to escape."

The first thing we did was send a message to our families because we couldn't go to them ourselves. We told them we had escaped and to expect the worst, because the military would be looking for us. We walked through the night and eventually found the home of the grandfather of Henry, one of my four colleagues. It was like a farm house, but deep in the bush around five miles outside Juba. We stayed for about four or five days, healing our bodies, resting and debating what to do next.

At the same time, the southern Sudanese had just started to flee and gather in Ethiopia because they were forced from their villages by the violence created by the soldiers from the North. The Ethiopian government welcomed the south Sudanese refugees into their country. All kinds of opposition groups were forming, but the most prominent cell was the Sudan People's Liberation Movement /Sudanese People's Liberation Army (SPLM/SPLA). This rebel group was formed by Sudanese soldiers who mutinied from the country's army in the city of Bor and decided to flee to Ethiopia too. The SPLM focused on the political agenda while the SPLA focused on the military initiative. Both the SPLM and the SPLA were under the effective leadership of Dr. John Garang.

The five of us who escaped from jail together discussed the idea of going to Ethiopia and although some thought that was a good idea, I felt it would be too dangerous to go at that time. The Ethiopian border was over 600 miles away, while the Congo border was just 150 miles away. I felt it was very unlikely we would make it to Ethiopia; it was a long walk and the whole south of Sudan was covered by soldiers who were blocking bridges over the river Nile. The Nile is a vast river infested with crocodiles and poisonous snakes, so we could not see making it across. Coming to

> The Nile is a vast river infested with crocodiles and poisonous snakes, so we could not see making it across.

the Congo was my idea. But there was some disagreement and we debated angrily because it was a critical decision that would affect our futures. I finally said, "Guys, the prime thing is to get out of Sudan and the nearest way is to go to the Congo border." So we made the walk through the bush, which took about five days. That was my last time in Sudan.

When we arrived at the border, the Congolese soldiers could not believe that we had come to the Congo to escape from Sudan – they had never even heard of refugees from south Sudan because the violence was so new. Indeed, we were the first of many who would come. My brother was working for the UN and had arranged safe transportation for us on a truck full of Ugandan refugees. (The many Ugandans who had fled to Sudan to escape the war in Uganda were now fleeing Sudan for Congo.) We explained to the soldiers at the border to Congo that we were political prisoners who had escaped, and they checked our story with those at the Sudanese UN office who verified that our lives were in danger. Right away, the Congolese took us in and gave us a place to live. They made a big mistake by first taking us to a refugee camp for Ugandans. These Ugandans had escaped Idi Amin's persecution and were afraid that, because we were non-Ugandans, we might be spies planted by the Amin government. Our lives were threatened in that camp, but we were lucky that the camp leaders were very reasonable. They listened to us and when they checked our belongings they discovered documents that helped explain our innocence. They also looked at our shoulders and found none of the marks soldiers develop from carrying guns. In the morning, the leaders told the UN office we were threatened and the UN staff moved us immediately to a small refugee hostel for those in transition.

The UN told us that our case was very strong: we had been persecuted, jailed and our lives had been threatened. They told us they would get us to safety as quickly as they could. We thought we would be taken to another African country, but it turned out they wanted to take us far away. Six months after arriving in the Congo, we were told that we were going to Canada. Just before leaving, I sent a message to my mom and dad. They came to Congo to say goodbye. We felt a sense of relief to know I was leaving Africa. I was going to a better country. My mom said, "Go and do something good for everyone if you can."

We were surprised to be going to Canada, because our prime interest then was to end up in Ethiopia. As we left Africa in late 1984, the circumstances in south Sudan were evolving into a major war. The government troops of the North were attacking southern villages, burning homes and crops, and kidnapping children. The natural resources from the rich farmlands of the South – tea, coffee, corn and oil – were being removed by hundreds and hundreds of trucks to northern Sudan. As well, millions of cattle were taken northwards with the goal of starving the people of the South. The international community's efforts to aid this famine were blocked by the northern government and millions died. The southern Sudanese continued to fear the northern Sudanese forces, so the village elders would tell people to leave the villages and walk east to Ethiopia. This is how the world came to hear of the *Lost Boys and Girls of Sudan*. Many, many children whose parents were killed in their villages walked eastward as much as 700 miles to reach Ethiopia.

They were fleeing their villages for safety. It was one of the greatest inhumanities of the twentieth century – little children forced to cross this wild territory unprotected. Those 150 miles I covered to get to the Congo were nothing in comparison to the 600 miles that tens of thousands of south Sudanese children had to walk. It is said that for every five children who fled, four did not reach Ethiopia.

Many of the Sudanese already in Ethiopia felt they could not sit back and continue in a peaceful way. Together the SPLM and SPLA were developing dominance as an opposing force against the northern Sudanese army. The SPLM advocated for the suffering of the southern Sudanese, while the SPLA was fighting the Arab dominated northern forces in the bush. Others stayed to volunteer in the refugee camps of Ethiopia, looking after the young Sudanese who had arrived from that terrible treacherous walk.

All five of us who had escaped prison together travelled to Winnipeg and began a new life here. Three friends have since moved to other Canadian provinces, and one has returned to Sudan. Today, I am the only one still in Winnipeg. I have been able to keep in touch with developments back home in southern Sudan. Even though there were no cell phones or Internet in 1984, gathering information was not a problem. I followed the news, and kept piles and piles of documents and every newspaper article I could get my hands on. When the Internet age came, that helped to provide me instantly with information. Over the years, some of the rebel leaders of southern Sudan have made global tours and stopped in Winnipeg to brief us on exactly what was going on.

In 2005, after twenty-two years of fighting, the Comprehensive Peace Agreement was signed. The Arab-dominated North had realized there was no way they were going to win the war. The SPLA had recaptured ninety-five percent of southern Sudan, confining the northern government troops to towns, so supplies could only come by planes, and a lot of northern soldiers were getting killed in the bush. One of the critical points of the Peace Agreement was the promise of a referendum in 2011. In that referendum the people of southern Sudan would vote to

> All five of us who had escaped prison together travelled to Winnipeg and began a new life here.

decide if they wanted their region to form an independent country. The referendum received ninety-eight percent support for independence. Following the referendum, the Republic of South Sudan gained its independence on July 9, 2011. For the first time, all south Sudanese – including myself – felt free at last from the tyranny of consecutive governments from the North. The current political climate is fragile but hopeful. Independence will not come easily because of the many issues South Sudan is faced with. However it is the hope of all south Sudanese that this step of independence will bring prosperity. I continue to follow the politics of South Sudan – it's in my blood

I have witnessed a lot of suffering. South Sudan is one of the poorest parts of the world because the resources have been exploited repeatedly by consecutive northern Sudanese governments. There is a lack of infrastructure, lack of sanitization, lack of proper education, no medical help and very few roads. People are still hungry and are still drinking dirty water. From that four-year-old boy who witnessed a catastrophic event in my village, I've become an adult who is passionately focused on contributing to my country.

I consider myself an activist who has campaigned very hard for the human rights of southern Sudan. I did not pick up the gun to kill anybody. It is, though, highly likely that had I stayed longer in Sudan, I would have been one of those involved in the violence. I think coming to Canada made me contribute to the politics of Sudan in a positive way. Many of my friends who picked up guns died a long time ago. I have lobbied very hard, writing letters to political leaders around the world.

My survival has been a blessing. I believe I have survived because of luck and determination. Sometimes on an escape route, I would manage to get through, or to get help, just when I was in danger of being captured. I don't know how to describe that, except to use the word "luck." I use the word "determination" because I never gave up. War is a terrible thing. It brings such disruption and destruction. Lives are lost that cannot be

> From that four-year-old boy who witnessed a catastrophic event in my village, I've become an adult who is passionately focused on contributing to my country.

brought back, and it takes the country back many years, so there is no progress, just misery and suffering.

Besides closely following the political developments in Sudan and now South Sudan, Akim volunteers with the Sudanese community in Winnipeg, works three jobs and still finds time to take courses at the University of Winnipeg. He is grateful to Canada for giving him safety and opportunity. He says his survival as a young boy in his village's attack has allowed him to be an ambassador for Sudan in Canada and to make a difference in the world.

MARCELINE

The approach to parenting I grew up with is parenting by fear,
but there is an alternative I think. It's parenting by love and negotiation.

I was born in Burundi in 1944. People in the culture I was raised loved children, but the children did not have rights. I like to say I was raised in a time when parents had rights and children did not have a say, but when I came to Canada in 1979, we brought our five children to a society where children had a lot of say and had to be listened to. As a parent, I joke – but there is some truth in it – *I* was not listened to! Somewhere along the way I missed my turn!

In 1972, I lived in India with my then husband and our five children because both my husband and I were attending the seminary there. At that time in Burundi, there was a selective genocide directed at Hutu intellectuals that claimed the lives of my pastor father, all five of my brothers and one of my two sisters. It is known now as a conspiracy of silence. My name was on a target list so the circumstances were such that we could not return to Burundi. Instead, we sought refugee asylum in Kenya.

We did receive asylum, and although there was not yet a refugee crisis or refugee camps like there are today, the conditions were not good. We could live there, but our family could never be citizens. We were surprised and disappointed to learn that at that time in Kenya there were no provisions to become a citizen for those who were not born there. Today, this is no longer the case, but at that time it meant we would be stateless forever, generation after generation.

We decided to apply to move to a country our children could at least call home. Another factor was that while in Kenya, we had no rights and a lot of restrictions. We could not own property, and the only jobs we could get were the ones that no Kenyans wanted to do, or if we were lucky, no Kenyans were qualified for. My husband was offered a very good job with a five-year contract, in a leadership role at a branch of the World Council of Churches, but if he'd taken that we would have been prevented from immigrating elsewhere, so he turned it down. It was a big sacrifice, but we wanted stability and a future for our children. That's why we came to Canada.

First we lived in Arcola, Saskatchewan, a small town southeast of Regina, and after that another small town, Lucky Lake. In 1984, my husband and I separated and I moved to Saskatoon. By 1985, the three oldest children were attending university while the two youngest were living with me. In 1992, I moved on my own to Northern Manitoba, and eventually Winnipeg.

As a child growing up in Burundi in the 1950s and '60s, I was disciplined by being physically hit. It was not just those in the Burundian culture who used physical force to discipline their children, it was common practice everywhere. It was also a philosophy many Christians believed at that time. The teaching was, "if you spare the rod you'll spoil the child." It was thought that spanking a child was appropriate "correction," an assurance that the child would stop doing something bad and be good. It was a common practice and common belief, and there were no questions asked. I recall as late as 1973 at the seminary in India, a professor, a very nice guy, saying that giving a good spanking to a kid was biblical; it was a good thing as long as there was an

> In 1992, I moved on my own to Northern Manitoba, and eventually Winnipeg.

explanation. That was a typical view at that time. I even recall a student in my daughter's high school in Lucky Lake as late as 1983 being given the strap for discipline. The school had to call the parents and they had to give permission.

But then a shift began: in the late 1970s and early '80s, there started to be discussion about discipline alternatives to physically hitting children. At the same time, women's liberation had become a strong movement. These ideas went hand in hand and both were resisted by tradition. When we came to Canada in 1979, it was a time of social change. I remember thinking that some parents were spoiling their children and many children were not well behaved. I did not know what to attribute that to. I do not recall attributing it to children not getting a spanking, I thought the parents were simply laissez-faire, too relaxed. On a personal level, I had been bothered by the lack of women's rights for many years. The equality that women in society were seeking, I had also wanted for myself. In this process, I came to consider that the kids might need their rights too, something that many women were advocating for. I think that's when I began to question

the idea of correcting a child physically and to think that maybe there was another way.

Before, I used to say to myself, *Well, I got spanked as a child, and I turned out all right.* But then I started looking back at my childhood more closely and I thought, *You know what ... I got those spankings for nothing.* This business of saying, "We hit you because we love you" is not right. One day, my oldest daughter and I were having an animated discussion. She was about sixteen at the time. I explained that my parents corrected by hitting, and we turned out all right. I gave her an example of a time my older brother stole something as a child and after a spanking, he did not do it again. Then my daughter said "Couldn't we say that you turned out all right *in spite* of that?" I thought about it and I said to myself, *That kid really does have a point.* She got me. She made a point I will never forget. And I started to think, *These are growing kids. Do I want a fear-based relationship? Do I want robots?* I want my kids to do good, because it is good to do good. My kids were ahead of my ideas, and I am thankful for that.

If I have one regret, I wish that before I had my children someone had taught me this: You do not have to hit children to discipline

them. There are other ways. You can negotiate with a child. You can use a method of positive reinforcement to encourage good behaviour and not dwell on the bad behaviour. I wish somebody had told me hitting does not have merit. I wish!

There is a huge adjustment for newcomers when arriving in Canadian culture. In my experience, many newcomers come from societies where striking a child is still acceptable. In many places violence is still sanctioned by the society and the culture, and it becomes an acceptable pattern. Men, being the physically stronger gender, control the women, who in turn control the children. Then boys, as they grow stronger than their fathers, come to protect their mothers. Those in control can and do use physical force to assert their authority. Sons see it and daughters see it, and the pattern is handed down. As well, in many countries there has been war and unrest. In climates like this, things do not change for the better, they become worse. In fact in circumstances such as these, children often become prey to even more violence; being raped and turned into child soldiers. Things are not getting better for children.

Still, there are many positive parenting behaviours from our home cultures, and we need to continue practicing them – keeping our children close to us, singing to them, listening to them and laughing with them. In Africa, parenting is a collective activity, whether you live in a home or in a refugee camp. For instance, when I had my first three children in Burundi, my mother-in-law did a lot (bless her heart) to raise the kids. Even people separated from their families will have a neighbour or an older woman who will do the parenting for them. Parents really depend on their extended family or the community. But so many things are different in Canada. Here, it becomes the mother and father, or just the mother raising the children. Very often, the father is not even part of it, because parenting has traditionally been seen as woman's work. It can be overwhelming to be the only one parenting.

Many of us from other cultures were used to giving the children rules and expecting them to be followed – no discussion. Often for refugees, there is a shortage of resources, so if children are smart, they will obey in order to survive (to get food for example). But then, children come to Canada and the parents are missing the extended family support I've spoken of, and parents struggle to get their children (particularly teenagers) to obey them. In Canada, there are other people in the community focused on the children's interest: in the schools, in government, and there are those who will listen more closely to the child. And here in Canada, children have laws to protect them. This can be good, but when immigrant children, teenagers especially, find they have rights, they may not understand them, and can even misuse them. For instance, if teens want to go out with their friends, or do something the parents would not approve of, the parents might try to hold them back from going out the door. This could be for the children's own good, but because the children know they cannot be hit, they can respond by saying that if the parents hold them, or even touch them, they will call 911. And they do.

For parents, it is a tough choice – let a child out the door to hang out on the downtown streets, or if the child is restrained and the parent and child struggle and a call goes

> In Africa, parenting is a collective activity, whether you live in a home or in a refugee camp.

out to 911, there is a chance the child will be removed from the home. Sometimes a child's claim of abusive treatment by the parent is based on truth, but sometimes it is not. I am lucky; I have never been in this situation. But I know it exists – I have seen it occur in other families. Parenting challenges are increased by other factors too: lack of positive role models for both parents and children, and the common newcomer stresses such as poverty, difficulty finding a good job, and settlement issues. Another big factor that is often overlooked is the lack of safe and affordable housing.

Schools are another important aspect. We need good schools with caring teachers who know the students by name and need and after-school programs such as open gym times in the evenings for families to play sports together. Many newcomer kids have also seen terrible things back home and have experienced trauma from war. They need extra programs and support. I see today the schools are working to improve their programs for new Canadians. Imagine being sixteen, not speaking English, coming to

> Many newcomer kids have also seen terrible things back home and have experienced trauma from war. They need extra programs and support.

Canada, and being expected to enter a Grade 11 classroom and begin to learn. These kids need help to catch up and should not be ignored. If they are not properly assisted their self-esteem becomes low, they may have trauma, and then they are vulnerable to gangs and drugs and street violence. If a child is struggling with these issues, parenting becomes even more difficult.

So how do parents who have used their hands to discipline get their kids to respect them without physical punishment? That's a big question. The approach to parenting I grew up with is parenting by fear, but there is an alternative I think. It's parenting by love and negotiation. Negotiation was a big part of parenting for me – after I came here, once I got it right.

There are so many good things we can do as parents. Listening is a big one. I remember when my youngest son was fourteen. I liked his group of friends, but he was often at their homes and wanting to stay late into the evening. When I asked him about it, he told me he was doing his homework on their computers because we did not have one at home. (I always appreciated that my kids were telling me the truth and I knew it). He was sitting in somebody else's basement waiting for a turn on the computer, and I knew this was going to harm his self-esteem. I thought that the best thing I could give my kids was a safe environment where they could do their schoolwork. Right around that time, my daughter was in university and she was having her own problems with the computer there. She came home very upset because she had written an essay on the university computer and at 10:00 p.m. when the lab was closing, the computer "ate" her essay and it was gone. I thought *Wow – now I have two unhappy children.* That was when I decided to buy a computer. It was the 1980s and computers were so expensive; ours cost $3,200. We had to make many sacrifices to buy one. I gave every penny I had to pay for it.

My daughter's problem ended well though. She had to hand in her essay at 10:00 a.m. the next morning. She got up early so she would arrive when the computer lab opened at 7:00 a.m. When she reached the lab … guess what? She found her older brother and two older sisters waiting there to help her. She had told

them her problem and they had all come to help her. None of them were living with us at the time. I don't know how they did it, but she handed that essay in on time. My children have always made a big effort to support each other. I am very proud of that.

After we got the computer, my son still wanted to go out with his friends. He was a teenager, and he and his friends just wanted to hang out having fun. I knew they were not doing anything bad and that I could trust my son. But at sixteen, he complained his curfew was too early. He said it was embarrassing if he had to leave earlier than everyone else when he was in the middle of hanging with his friends or at a party. So that's when we negotiated. I used to tell my kids, *don't yell – negotiate.* If they have a reason, I will listen and if I'm wrong I will accept that. If we reach an impasse, I will have the last word because I am responsible for them and must protect them. My son told me he felt he was a responsible person and I agreed. I felt I needed to respect what he was saying, so we came up with a solution based on compromise. He would request a curfew based on the context of each evening's plans. No matter what, all my kids knew they had to phone home if they were delayed. It was about safety and communication.

I once had a friend come to me stressed out because he could not buy many things for his eight-year-old son. I said "No problem. You don't need to buy him something. Do you have $3? Go and hold your boy's hand and say *today you have a date with me*, a time that you set aside just for him." The next day the father came back to me and said it was amazing. Spending time with our children is like magic. As my children grew and life was full of more disruptions, we would celebrate EVERYTHING, just to have an excuse to make more time together. If we did it, we celebrated it! We would laugh and sit around the dinner table. My children have told me those simple times together were some of the best. One of my sons wrote this in a letter to me, "My memories are of spending time together and of joy and laughter. For example, cleaning endless piles of laundry by hand, all the time laughing and telling stories." That goes a long way – laughing at ourselves. Humour is very helpful. It is not for everyone, but it comes naturally for me and my children.

> If I were to give advice today to my younger self, I would say that the principles of parenting should be love in action.

Humility also plays a big part in parenting. Usually, parents think they are going to lose face by admitting their mistakes, but it is not true; it is the opposite. Paradoxically, if parents admit their errors and show they are human, it goes a long way. It sets a good example that we do not have to be perfect. I once invited someone for Christmas dinner when my children and I were all together for the holidays. My daughter heard me on the phone and when I got off, she said "We have only a little time together as a family; you did not ask us about this guest. We want a quiet Christmas together. It's our day." They stood their ground. They had a point; some had come from far away, and they were looking forward to this day together. They should have a say in it. I said "You are right; I did not consult you. I had better cancel that invitation and do it fast!" I thought to myself at that moment, *After ten or twenty years, I am still making mistakes … and I have to correct them.*

If I were to give advice today to my younger self, I would say that the principles of parenting should be love in action. Choosing not to hit a child is not being wishy-washy. There are other choices. You cannot hit a child and then say I love you. It is misguided. And you must always communicate to them over and over that you love, love, love LOVE, LOVE, LOVE, LOVE them.

Marceline's children are grown now. All five have received university degrees and are well settled. One was even named an Oxford Rhodes Scholar. Marceline says that what she cares about most is that all are kind human beings with social consciences. In celebration of her sixtieth birthday, each of her children wrote her a letter about her impact on them. They were words of love and deep respect, describing her strength and sense of humour, her "kindness to a fault" and "generosity of spirit." Marceline is quick to point out that she felt she had good kids, saying that "although at times they acted just like every other kid, not wanting to do the housework and so forth, it was not what I did as a parent (well, maybe a little bit) it was the positive good nature of our kids."

At age sixty-eight, Marceline has a lifetime of stories and insights. Originally, she

declined to participate in this book because she wants to write about them herself. But one day, Marceline and I had the occasion to speak about parenting – always a popular topic – especially for immigrants. Her wisdom was quickly evident. I asked her to reconsider being in the book and am grateful to her for sharing her wisdom in this piece. I thank her especially for her honesty on an often-private topic.

DEBORAH

When I came to Winnipeg I had a deep sense of knowing that this was where I belonged.

I cannot talk about my life without talking about my faith. I am a pastor, and before that I was a pastor's daughter. Sure, I had a time in my twenties when I had to move from seeing God as the God of my father to making a choice to take Him as my personal God, but I have lived my entire life in faith. I came to Canada from Nigeria in 1986, not because of fear or violence but as part of my call to study theology.

Thankfully, Nigeria has not gone through war in recent times, so most Nigerians come to Canada in pursuit of better lives and better education. Although our past is not of war or disaster, we as immigrants have our own stories to share. Our lives have been impacted by our choice to move to Canada. God, through Canada, made my dreams of education and ministry come true.

My childhood in Nigeria was both eventful and joyful. I am the youngest of six children. My parents were ministers in the Nigerian branch of the Evangelical Missionary Church of Canada (EMCC, but known as UMCA), an offshoot of the Mennonite Church. My father was trained and mentored by missionaries from Canada, and my parents served God until their deaths. So as children, we were born into the church life. My father pastored in many churches throughout the district, moving every three to five years, as was common practice.

My life was eventful because we moved from one town to another, meeting all kinds of people. My love of travelling and making new friends, and my levels of tolerance and acceptance, all come from these early experiences. They taught me to love adventure. As a school-age girl in my country, I was able to live beyond usual ethno-cultural boundaries. It was a rich cultural experience for me. I was exposed at an early age to what would become mission for me as an adult. My life was also eventful because my mother died when I was six years old. Yes, we had a crisis losing our mom, but it was our faith and our family that helped us through. At age eleven, when my oldest sister Mary got married, I moved in with her and her husband. It is a cultural thing in my country that when a woman is married and leaves her father's house, the family sends a younger sibling along as a little helper, so that the woman will not be lonely. Having a familiar face from our families is a way of gradually easing us into married life. Because I was the youngest, Mary had stepped into the role of mother for me at the time of our mom's death. So it was more natural for me to want to go and live with Mary when she married than to stay with my father and his new wife.

My childhood was joyful because, even though we did not have much materially, we had the love of our family. For any African, family is everything, and we are strong community people. My childhood was joyful because my father was there. He had a beautiful father's heart; nothing kept him too busy to care for me. After my mother died, and before he remarried, I travelled with him as he worked in various locations. I was really a big part of his daily life. We were very close.

> My love of travelling and making new friends, and my levels of tolerance and acceptance, all come from these early experiences. They taught me to love adventure.

He gave me his best, and although I missed my mom, there was never a dull moment to really, really miss her. I was given everything – not in terms of material things, but emotionally. That really solidified my growing up.

It is a Nigerian Christian tradition that when babies are born, they are named on their eighth day. They remain at home with their mothers while their parents pray over them and ask God to protect them. Then on the fortieth day, the families take the babies to church and have celebrations where the children are dedicated. My father told me that when I was dedicated the Lord told him and my mom that they were holding an evangelist. During those years when I was a young adult, my father sometimes had reason to question whether this prophecy would come true. At that time, I did not want to be involved with church as much as my parents had been. As a pastor's child I wanted to be a good person, but I didn't want to feel pressured into participating just because someone else thought I should be. I guess I was just acting my age. But also, some aspects of our lives had been difficult, with people picking on us because we were a pastor's children, expecting us to be perfect, and almost asking us not to be human.

In my early twenties, I had wanted to become a pilot. I went for an interview, but the man I was supposed to see was on vacation, and my meeting was rescheduled. The following week I was involved in a serious car accident. The car was totaled; however, I walked away with fewer injuries than expected. The third day after my accident, I had a revelation while staying at my sister Mary's home. It was there in the middle of the night that I saw the Lord in my dream. He was in the figure of a tall man in dazzling, blinding white. He spoke to me, saying that he had been waiting for me for a long time, but the stubbornness of my heart had kept me from him. He then picked me up and put me on his lap and comforted me. This powerful experience changed everything for me. I never went back to that rescheduled interview to become a pilot.

Instead, I enrolled at the UMCA Theological College in Ilorin, Nigeria. I met a person at the College who later became a great and close friend, Barbara Sparks, a Canadian from Kitchener, Ontario, who was teaching there. Back in the 1980s, most of the students were married men with wives accompanying them. I was different. I was the first single girl from my denomination UMCA (United Missionary Church of Africa), attending a Bible College to become a preacher. Before my arrival, there was one other single missionary woman, Lois Fuller (now Lois Dow), who had been praying for a girl to come to the school to be in the Lord's women ministry. So, my presence there was an answer to her prayer.

My dad must have been overjoyed that the earlier revelation that I would serve the Lord as a minister was finally coming true. He even saw me preach once. It was my first preaching assignment in my home church during a visit back home while I was a student at the Bible School in Ilorin. I was very nervous to be preaching in front of him, so that morning, before church service, I asked him to pray with me and release a blessing upon me. He had such joy while he prayed over me that my fear of making a mistake vanished. As I began preaching, I focused on depending on the Holy Spirit, and the Lord took over. Afterwards, I remember my father extended his hand to me and said, "Welcome to the

> My dad must have been overjoyed that the earlier revelation that I would serve the Lord as a minister was finally coming true.

ministry." We became prayer partners that day, agreeing to pray for whatever the other needed. That was powerful for me.

I knew the Lord wanted me to attend theology school, but the denomination at that time did not know what to do with me! So when I met Barbara and Lois, both single, we three developed a close bond. They were women ahead of me on the road who could mentor and encourage me. Barbara returned to Canada while I was in my third year of college, but we kept in contact. After I completed my fourth and final year, Barbara suggested I come to Canada and continue my studies there. Nigeria was originally under British rule, so my education had all been in English. This knowledge of the language made coming to Canada easier.

In June 1986, my application to Emmanuel Bible College in Kitchener was accepted. The EMCC gave me a scholarship and agreed to pay for my schooling. I was excited to travel, but it was my first time travelling overseas. My father encouraged me to go, but I wondered if I would ever see him again. Still, I had a real sense of peace because Barbara would be there to meet me. At the time, I thought my life in Canada would be easy, with no stress and the chance to make money quickly. I thought there would be only good people and everyone would be Christian. But of course I was naive.

On the day of my departure to Canada, my father took me to the airport. We sat together in the back seat of his car, while his driver drove the three-hour journey from our town. My father tried to tell me everything he could possibly think of. I remember he gave me a Bible and one of his preaching robes – it was deep purple. He said, "This is the best thing I can give you". He gave me money too, knowing I would need it. I cried and cried. When we could see the airport in the distance, he stopped the car. He told me I should take public transport the rest of the way. I think this was his way of releasing me and giving me my own independence. I also think it was just too emotional for him – with his baby girl, his youngest and most adventurous, leaving. I can still see him looking back at me. His eyes showed me he had mixed feelings – worry about what my future would hold and whether we would see each other again,

but also tremendous pride. We didn't have any cell phones back then, but we wrote back and forth. I also made a number of trips back to Nigeria after that day of separation and, fortunately, did get to see my father before he passed away in 2000.

Barbara met me at the airport in Toronto, and I knew I was in good hands. I began to meet people at both school and church. I was impressed with their generosity. My early years in Canada as a student were fun. I like to say my Caucasian friends taught me all the bad things I know! I was blessed with good friends who walked me through that transitional time. I even met one of the missionaries my father had worked with, Reverend Willis Hunkings, and his wife Marion. He was the promotions manager for Emmanuel Bible College, so his job was to go from church to church in Southern Ontario and Michigan telling people about our school and recruiting students. I had a good work ethic and I always finished my schoolwork quickly, so on weekends I began to get involved in missions and travel with him. "Come snow or come rain, as long as

the roads are open," he would say, "I'll get you there." His own children were grown and gone from home, so I came into his life at just the right time. I used to call him Dad. He was a man of faith and used to just pour his knowledge into me. Apparently, he and Marion saw something in me that I did not see in myself at the time. He gave me many opportunities to speak at churches we visited.

So for me, apart from the colour of the people, it was a life I was used to.

In the 1980s in Kitchener, there were very few black people. The ones I did see were most often from the Caribbean. Because I was a black African woman, people were curious about me, and that gave me a platform to share my faith. People were so surprised I had come all the way to Canada to study theology because of my faith. But this special notice by people also made me realize that I was standing on a delicate stage: people were watching to see how I lived my life. People were waiting to see if the influences of the Western world and my newfound freedom would affect my faith. But I knew where I had come from and that

My early years in Canada as a student were fun. I like to say my Caucasian friends taught me all the bad things I know!

it would cost too much to walk away from the Lord. That helped me refine my faith and strengthen my convictions.

At the time I was attending Bible College, my sister Grace was living with her husband in Brooklyn, New York. She had been there since she was married in the 1970s. They helped support me by paying my room and board in the college dormitory. (When I needed spending money I would work in the kitchen at the Bible College.) During my school holidays I would go to visit my sister in Brooklyn. While there, I met a group that was worshipping and studying the Bible together. The man who had begun the group had just moved back to Nigeria, so I stepped in and began leading them.

From those visits, the Lord used us to help start a church there. I am an explorer and I like to start new things. So for six years, during my years of study and after, I led the church as I travelled back and forth. I was heavily committed to the congregation because I wanted to see the church grow. Those years were good training for me. But I did not feel that the Lord was calling me to

live in New York City, nor was he calling me to pastor that church. God was very specific about the way He was leading me. I was there as the "traveling" pastor until they hired an older couple who took the church to another level. This feeling influenced other choices I made about my pastoring.

After I received my Bachelor of Theology degree from Emmanuel Bible College, I took a year off to work with street kids, with youth suffering mental illness, and at a group home. I also continued helping at my church in Kitchener and being involved in missions. Then Barbara and I started talking about my doing a master's degree. I applied to Providence College and Seminary in Winnipeg and to two other schools in the United States. But as I indicated earlier, I did not feel the Lord leading me to the States. One of the US schools was affiliated with Emmanuel Bible College where I had received my undergrad degree, and everyone at Emmanuel wanted me to go there. But when I told Rev. Hunkings that I did not feel called to that school, he said he trusted me and trusted God to lead me where I was

> I took a year off to work with street kids, with youth suffering mental illness, and at a group home.

meant to be. I am grateful he understood. I prayed that if it was Providence College and Seminary, I should attend then their admissions letter would be the first to come through – that would be evidence. Sure enough, the Providence letter arrived first. That gave me confidence in my choice.

So I left Kitchener for Winnipeg in 1991. My church community in Kitchener introduced me to a church in Winnipeg, Heritage Fellowship. Pastor Denis Anderson was waiting to connect with me. I remember calling him to get driving instructions into Winnipeg, and when I arrived it was Sunday morning, so I drove straight to the church. I became involved in the church on the pastoral team and did the internship portion of my master's degree in Christian Education under his supervision.

One particular day I was in the church's sanctuary, praying, and the Lord said to me, a day would come when I would pastor a different kind of congregation here in this building. Then in 1995, Pastor Anderson moved to another church and the board of Heritage Fellowship asked me to become the new pastor. But I told them the Lord had not called me to pastor Heritage Fellowship and the timing was not right. I was settled in my heart and certain that the Lord had meant another congregation. For it was specifically impressed upon my heart that the congregation would first be an ethnic group of Nigerians and later become an international church. The members of the board were surprised and could not understand. They wondered why I wouldn't step in as pastor, but I felt the Lord had said something else to me. I continued to be seriously involved at the church, doing every other thing but preaching. I arranged for guest pastors until the arrival of the new pastor, Mike, a friend and classmate of mine from Emmanuel in Kitchener. I felt that to step in and become the pastor of Heritage would have been a deliberate act of disobedience to the Lord.

It was during that time, while I was supporting and worshipping at Heritage Fellowship, and with the approval and blessing of Pastor Mike, that I came to begin Immanuel Fellowship congregation in the

> I remember calling him to get driving instructions into Winnipeg, and when I arrived it was Sunday morning, so I drove straight to the church.

same building, but with a service at a different time. The first members were a family I had come to know from babysitting their son. We had become good friends and had started a Bible study group together. Other Nigerians heard about our group and joined us. Africans are prayer warriors, so while Mike was pastoring Heritage and offering services Sunday mornings, I still faithfully attended his morning service. Our Bible study group also began to worship in the same building, offering Sunday afternoon services, under the name Immanuel Fellowship Church.

It is important to me to integrate African and Canadian cultures.

Once every month, the two congregations worshipped together. All the tithes and offering collected during the weekly worship services of Immanuel Fellowship were handed over to Heritage, then our senior sister church. Eventually Pastor Mike and his family moved out west and the Heritage Fellowship congregation began to dwindle. Many people were moving on. In the meantime, the Immanuel Fellowship congregation was growing. Eventually the afternoon offerings collected became the main financial support for the church building, and Heritage

Fellowship Church disbanded. Because both churches were under the EMCC, Heritage Church left the building in the caring hands of Immanuel Fellowship leadership. We just kept growing and growing.

During the early days of Immanuel Fellowship, I was volunteering my time at the church while working full time as a hospital chaplain at the Health Sciences Centre (HSC). That was a very good job, because it helped me to learn about local culture and how to minister to the people. It is important to me to integrate African and Canadian cultures. The Lord blessed me with the gift of dreams, and, at that time, he told me in a dream that my time at HSC was coming to an end. The church was growing and there was need for a full-time minister. So in 1997, when my position at HSC was up for renewal and I was asked to re-apply, I decided to resign voluntarily. I saw it as an opportunity to work permanently at Immanuel Fellowship. As well, at that time I returned to Providence College and Seminary to enroll in the Doctorate of Ministry program. EMCC financially supported our church as it was still considered a new church. I knew God was calling me to be a prophet away from home, to my people. Today, the church congregation is ninety-nine percent African.

In the meantime, I was praying for a husband, a man who would love people and would not suppress the gift of God in me. God has blessed me with just such a wonderful husband in Sunday Akinola. He allows me to do what he has come to believe is my destiny – helping people. We are thankful to have two beautiful sons, Israel and John, born in 1999 and 2000.

In my denomination, I was the first woman both in Nigeria and Canada to complete a Doctor of Ministry program. My story was very important to my denomination. It was during my era that the EMCC denomination had to seriously look at female ordination. I was their Godly blessed guinea pig. They could not deny the Lord's call upon my life, and yet they did not know what to do with me. There was never a time when I fought for my own ordination; instead, I watched as those leading EMCC leaders wrestled with how to approach it. I have a deep respect for them; they chose to walk in obedience and honour my call. If they had told me I could not preach or share my faith, and that I

was only meant to make blankets and cookies that would have crushed me.

In 1995, EMCC gave me my license; the first female. And finally in 2003, I was ordained. The waiting was not hard though, because it was not me who had a problem with the issue, but a few men in the denomination. I felt they needed time to work through things, and I would rather put my energy into doing what God has called me to do in my daily life than use energy to fight for something I am convinced God is in charge of delivering. I continued to pray that God would help me to obey Him as I waited. My patience came from the Lord, because I had a deep sense of peace that I was doing not only the right thing, but also the Godly thing. I did not allow human limitations or a set of rules to control me.

The day of my ordination brought a sense of the denomination's affirmation of my own call to ministry. But I knew God had already called me long ago, and all I needed from them was their affirmation that I was called to serve God through our denomination, EMCC.

When I came to Winnipeg, I had a deep sense of knowing that this was where I belonged. Sometimes there are moments in our lives when the circumstances just click into place, and we know something beyond doubt. I feel at home here. I love the prairies and the open sky. My favourite thing to do is to drive out into the open country fields at night in the fall. I love to watch the stars. The ultimate for me is to see the Northern Lights. Sitting alone in those fields, I can forget myself in the presence of God. The flat prairies are similar to northern Nigeria where I did a lot of missionary work. I actually came from a city with a lot of mountains surrounding it, but I did not like those mountains; I felt closed in by them and wanted to see beyond. I am a person who does not like limitations – I like to spread my wings. I used to pray, *Please God do not send me to* BC!

Winnipeg people … what can I say? It's friendly Manitoba! I think this is because Winnipeg has immigrant roots: people from all over – Ireland, Ukraine, Germany. There is openness here to people and culture. There is something in the Manitoba culture that attracts people here to those who have just arrived, as if it's in Manitoba's genes to be kind to visitors and to help and respond to immigrants because that is the foundation of Manitoba. The fact that Manitoba is a leading province in Canada for the immigration process is not a surprise.

Sure, every immigrant experiences racism one time or another. However, the way it is handled is what matters. I experienced racism while working as a hospital chaplain, but I chose to see that not as my problem; rather, it was the problem of the other person. I just let it go. Many things have improved for immigrants and Africans since the 1980s. In the 1980s, Africans were looked upon suspiciously as people who had come to Canada to acquire the nation's wealth and resources, as those who did not know anything and had nothing to contribute to the community. But things are so much better now. International immigrants have come to study and in recent years, with compassionate aid to refugees, there are now more and more immigrants. Manitoba has risen to the occasion understanding that these are not "come and go people" but people coming to stay and to contribute.

> The flat prairies are similar to northern Nigeria where I did a lot of missionary work.

Manitoba has become more diverse so there are more programs and training for immigrants. All of this is an effort on the part of the people of Manitoba to do better. There is a sincere desire to understand cultures that are now on our doorsteps. I am convinced that policies have changed and will continue to change. This blending and integrating are very important because even in our small Manitoba we have the world. I want to be used as a bridge between the African and Canadian cultures. We are the most blessed, as immigrants and as a province, if we can tap into both cultures.

If you ask me today, am I Nigerian or am I Canadian, I would say that I am a woman first, and also that I am not limited. I am Canadian by citizenship and Nigerian by heritage. I am a diverse woman of rich culture whose mind has been expanded in order to understand my world better. When I gave birth to our eldest son, it dawned on me that this was going to be the place we put down our family roots; then Canada really felt like home. Sometimes I am asked if I feel lucky; my answer is that I do not believe in luck. I am blessed. Why am I blessed? I am blessed in order to bless other people and share my life. When I observe all that God has done through me, and for me, I feel very humbled. I want my legacy to be a legacy of passion and compassion, of faithfulness and of giving back to a community that has given me so much, all because of God. I am extremely grateful.

> If you ask me today, am I Nigerian or am I Canadian, I would say that I am a woman first, and also that I am not limited.

Deborah expressed tremendous gratitude for Canada and the opportunities the country has given her. She says her early experience here was so positive that she vowed she would make her home available to international students regardless of colour, race, ethnicity or country. She has been hosting University of Manitoba students since 1991. She and her husband now open their home to new Canadians while they first settle here. Deborah told me that the best thing Canadians can do to help immigrants after they arrive is to be a real, genuine friend. She added that immigrants are community people looking for friendships that are transparent, based on honesty and direct conversation.

Deborah says, "immigrants are resilient and hard working and they will do almost anything to make sure that their dreams do not die." She believes that Canada is the perfect place for realizing these dreams. She and her husband try to pass on this principle to the new Canadians they meet.

ANONYMOUS

That is my fight – for the recognition of the refugee as a human being. How wonderful it would be, to be part of a society that has truly received us, confirming that our humanity exists.

I wish I could have come to Canada as a tourist, but I came here as a refugee to escape from the violence happening in my country. Yes, I experienced war, and it tried to destroy some part of me, but I survived and have kept my humanity. My identity is not just about war and suffering: before the war I was someone.

I had a profession as a teacher, a family and dreams for our future. Then war shattered my entire life. Next came fear, separation from my family and unemployment. Thank God Canada – a foreign country to me – accepted me as a newcomer and protected me. But I felt like I was being born once more, that I was weak and dependent like a child, having to relearn everything. Now, I want to have an identity separate from the war. Being defined by war is very heavy and I don't want to carry that. I want happiness in my new country. And already, although I never chose to live here, I have come to love this place.

I came from the Democratic Republic of Congo, which used to be called Zaire. It is a country that has been at war for many decades now. The trouble lies in the eastern part of Congo, where I lived – close to the Ugandan border. The fighting there has been between two tribes: the Hema and Lendu. Over 5,000,000 people have died because of this war. I have lost seven members of my family including my sister and uncle. As a result of the war, I started to work with a group of women, mothers from both tribes who were secretly trying to protect their children, as young as ten years old, from being enrolled as child soldiers in the armies. The authorities became aware that I was working with these women, so I was arrested and spent ten months in jail. I was released with the help of a friend who was a Catholic priest. When he learned I was in prison, he managed to collect some money together for a bribe and to talk the authorities into releasing me. Once free, I immediately crossed into Uganda where I made my way to Canada in 2005. I came for my safety.

I had never heard of Manitoba before. This priest friend had once visited Winnipeg in the 1970s and knew a few people here. That type of connection always makes it a bit easier to start somewhere.

I came alone. I had two daughters and a wife, but they are not with me in Canada. When I was imprisoned, it was my prayer that they were alive, so as soon as I escaped from jail I asked where they were. According to my priest friend, they had fled safely to Uganda. I was told to focus first on my safety and then try to communicate with my family later. Once in Canada, with the help of the International Red Cross Network, I learned they were in Europe. When I contacted my wife she did not believe it was me; fourteen months had passed since we had last seen each other. She had thought I was dead, and could not believe I was alive. Once I had made contact with my family, I began the application process for them to come to Canada so we could be together again. Only then did I learn that when my wife thought I was dead, she had started a new life with a man who was very kind to her when she and the girls had first

> I came alone. I had two daughters and a wife, but they are not with me in Canada.

arrived. She said she was pregnant with his child and that she and my daughters would not be coming to be with me in Canada. She had not been able to bring herself to tell me sooner. She was afraid of what the shock could do to me.

I thought of going to live closer to my girls, but immigration in Europe is very complicated, and moving to a new country to begin yet again would have been very difficult for me. I spent months not answering my wife's calls. I was angry and frustrated and that was destroying me. I started to rethink things. I knew I had to find peace with this situation or I could not live my life the way I wanted to. So finally, I called her and we began talking again. I started to see that it was not her fault that this whirlwind happened. Before I was arrested, my wife used to warn me that my actions against the war could cause us danger. But it's not my fault either because I had to act on my convictions. I did realize, though, that I needed forgiveness from her just as much as she did from me. Now, I can forgive and I can understand. She is the mother of my girls, and before being the mother of my girls, she

> As a father, if I say I am okay with not having my family with me, I am lying. I do not spend one day without thinking about my girls.

was the lady that I loved. I want to keep our friendship and to have peace in my heart again.

As a father, if I say I am okay with not having my family with me, I am lying. I do not spend one day without thinking about my girls. But I have come to realize this is not just my story; thousands and thousands of other refugees are going through similar experiences. Becoming separated and developing lives apart is not an uncommon refugee experience. I believe it is important that anyone who deals with refugees knows there is a great price we have paid that can never be fully understood by those who haven't had to flee their home countries and become separated from family members.

When I arrived in Canada the world was talking a lot about what happened in the United States on September 11, 2001. That day about 3,000 people died, and today the world is still shaken by this tragedy. But there are not 3,000 people dying there every day; they died on only that one day. In Congo, more than five million innocent people have lost their lives by guns and violence. Daily, innocent women are raped and children are taken into the army. Let us talk about their safety. Are the world and its leaders willing to stop that? For me, this is a real hypocrisy. It is my hope that the common people of our society will never give up and will continue to ask world leaders, *What are you doing about the wars?*

Canada receives many refugees. When we come, we do not arrive with peace of mind. Instead, we come with baggage, the baggage of suffering and that creates an image that influences how Canadians see us. This is one of the big challenges of being a refugee. But it is a mistake to presume we have nothing to contribute to this country because of our personal history of suffering. I think there is miscommunication and misunderstanding between us refugees and the local Canadian communities here. New refugees expect the community to understand them, but unless the refugee life is explained, the community cannot be aware. I also believe it is very important for Canadians to learn about the refugees who have come here, to ask, *How do you live in your country? How do people talk to each other?* And not to say, *You are here now, forget about your way of living and embrace the Canadian way.* That

creates frustration. Adding to the problem is the community's expectation that the refugee should adjust quickly to a new way of life without any prior experience of it. Canadians might say, *We are helping you to come over, why don't you respect our advice? Your ways are not the way you are supposed to live. THIS is the way you are supposed to be.* And the refugee might say, *You don't want to understand us.* This is a clash of culture and identity. I understand both sides – the views of the community that wants to support the refugee but also the needs of the refugee starting a new life. I think patience and awareness are very important.

Let me share a common refugee experience. A newcomer is at a job interview. In Canadian culture it is important to look someone in the eyes. But for the newcomer, it is disrespectful in his home country to do this. He wants to give the employer respect, so he looks away. This makes the employer think he is hiding something so the employer does not give him the job. The newcomer thinks he did not get the job because he was not liked. He believes he was respecting the employer, but the employer does not know this. That is a type of misunderstanding that refugees have to deal with.

I believe that people in Manitoba like helping and are willing to help, but I think "how to help," that is where the challenge is. Some people confuse helping with telling someone what they should do. There can be an attitude of superiority: *You are the one who needs me and my country because you are coming here.* This does not help us. For me, helping is based on respect and an understanding of each other. To say, *I don't have anything to learn from you; you are the one learning from me* creates the impression of inferiority. If we don't courageously learn about each other, we will find ourselves in the position of master and slave. We might be scared to call it that, but let's call it by its name. As newcomers, we sometimes hear the message; *You don't have anything to give.* Some individuals may not say this, but their actions show us.

As refugees, we continuously risk losing our identity. When we come here, to this new country we call home, yes, we come needy and weak, but we do not want to stay stuck in dependency on others. We want to become fully mature as Canadians and as human beings. And we see a difference between short-term and long-term help. With the large number of refugees coming to Canada, people say they would like to give a cup, or a bed or a television. They really care. That is a good start, but I believe help like that is for the short term. You can buy me a bed, a huge beautiful bed, but if I cannot sleep, then it is just for decoration. I know that it was not meant for decoration, it was meant for sleep, but in order for me to be able to have a restful sleep I need to feel like a contributing, valuable member of the society I live in.

Some people confuse helping with telling someone what they should do.

I believe we should put into practice the Chinese philosophy of fishing. Instead of always giving me fish, show me how to fish. Then we can fish together and share our fish, or I can bring you fish tomorrow. Why not see my way of catching fish? You are good at catching fish in the cold but where I come from it is hot, and we know how to catch fish in the sun and in the rain. Maybe I can show you my tricks and we can learn from each other. This approach gives us opportunities for the future. During my years of growing up, my father used to say, *Please ask one another how can we work together.* When you start to think of things that way, people are drawn together because they feel comfortable. They sense wisdom. The secret is to ask, *How can we work together?* and not to say, *Listen to me; this is how it should be.* Despite our suffering as refugees, we are still part of humanity. That is my fight – for the recognition of the refugee as a human being. How wonderful it would be, to be part of a society that has truly received us, confirming that our humanity exists.

I believe that all refugees have a responsibility to make the community aware of these views and desires and to work to change the stigmas they encounter. If we start to think we have nothing to give, that is dangerous because we would become full of doubt and not be strong. Then it would be harder to offer ourselves to the community, to participate and produce. As newcomers in Canada, we need to find the courage to embrace our new country and the opportunities we have here. Despite the challenges we faced back home, we need to rediscover what we can each uniquely offer to the world, stay true to this part of ourselves, and share it. Doing

> If we start to think we have nothing to give, that is dangerous because we would become full of doubt and not be strong.

just that has helped me heal, and returned my sense of identity. This is my message of hope to each newcomer.

When I came to Canada, I purposefully decided not to become part of a cycle of dependence. I decided to have courage and to see my life as a light. Whatever I went through can make me stronger. I have decided not to be a negative person, but to look for happiness and to let myself live that happiness now. I have started a new life; I have a wonderful supportive lady and we have a beautiful child together. But if you ask me what my one dream is, it is to be together with my two daughters again. What have my girls done in this world to be without their father? As a teacher, I sometimes get the opportunity to work with kids. They are so amazing, so beautiful to watch. But I am a realist and know that I cannot live with my girls in the way I wish: to hug them, to take them to the park or the theatre, to hear them crying, to carry them, even to see them do something naughty. You know I miss that.

I believe I have something to share with the world, something of benefit to give, just as I have been given so much here. I am trying little by little to help educate others about what refugees are going through, and also to help refugees take advantage of the opportunities we have here. I wonder if maybe one day my daughters will ask me *Why was it Dad that we were not together?* That question eats at my mind. I could say that it was because of the war, but what is "the war?" I believe that war is selfishness, a selfishness that does not belong to just one race or group; it belongs to each of us. When we refuse to share and refuse to support each other, then we go to war. Maybe by showing that I have overcome my experiences of loss as a refugee and have therefore been able to help others and further understanding and respect in the world, I will have some kind of answer for my daughters.

This man carries himself with a fierce dignity that originates from deep respect for the world, and for himself. His passion is for us all to discover what we uniquely have to offer, and in doing so, to empower ourselves to be our best for others. This is not just a message for victims of war, but also victims of abuse,

poverty and injustice. He has requested anonymity, because even though he is thousands of miles and a number of years away from his homeland, he does not feel safe. Having spoken out in the past, while living in Canada, he has received hateful email threats and members of his family back home have been violently beaten. It is not uncommon for outspoken refugees to be stalked via the Internet. He says "the challenges of war follow you everywhere."

ASUMANI

As a refugee I had had years of just going and going.
When you live the life of having nothing and moving around,
it became the only life I knew how to live.

When I was a little boy about eight, my mother told me about the secret of the signs. That was in Rwanda in 1994, right before the genocide began. She told me that there was fighting now in our country, just like in Burundi in 1972 and 1986. She remembered how those wars separated families and how people disappeared. Children ran, escaping from Burundi to Congo or Rwanda or Tanzania.

So when she saw that war was beginning in 1994, she explained to us that each of us children had our own individual signs or marks on our bodies. She told me that if we were ever separated and then met again, I should remember her by the markings on her face – dark spots like freckles, but raised like moles. She said she would remember me

by the mole on the inside middle finger of my right hand. She explained, "We might be separated for ten or twenty years, you children might be grown up already and I would be an old woman. You will not remember what I look like, but if you remember the sign it will help us." Years later, I would use this secret of the sign to recognize my mother in a market in Tanzania.

I was born in 1986 in Bujumbura, the capital of Burundi. I was the fifth of nine children, but we are only six now. Two of my brothers died when they were infants and my oldest brother, Musa, was shot and killed when he was a teenager and I was still young. Even though I was born in Burundi, I spent only about one month of my life there. At the time of my birth, the rest of my family was living in Rwanda. My mother – pregnant with me – had been travelling to Burundi to buy the clothes that she sold in the markets in Rwanda. She decided to stay there with extended family instead of travelling back on the roads. She was worried she would miscarry because of the bumpiness of the transportation. My family first left Burundi for Congo in 1972. That was the beginning of the Hutu genocide. Although my parents were not Hutu or Tutsi, many were dying and they felt unsafe and left. But life was not easy in the Congo so in 1974 they moved on to the big capital city of Kigali in Rwanda. My mother was born in Congo and my father in Burundi. My brother Musa was born there too, but all my other siblings were born in Rwanda. My father worked as a mechanic there and my mother had a business selling food, clothing, and TV antennas in the market. In 1989, my father passed away from a tumour in his stomach. I do not remember him because I was so young when he died, but my older sisters Feza and Mariamu remember my father. I have one old black-and-white photo of my family before I was born. In it are my dad and mom. It was a long time ago.

My clear memories of my childhood are only of my mother. She told us that before my father died, they talked together about us children. He asked her to look after us. My mother made that promise and she did everything she could to live up to that promise. My mother never had another husband. She struggled to make money for us. She worked really hard. She began selling mangos in the market as a small girl, so she had good experience as a business woman. She sold gold from Congo and African clothing from Burundi. She also bought fruit and had us children sell it in the local markets. We would bring the money back to her.

In Africa, they say that you are as rich as the number of children you have, because they work for the family, not like in Canada where it seems that you are as poor as the number of children you have because there is much more here to want and children are given so much: university, computers, iPods, cell phones. In Africa, it is common for children as young as seven or ten years old to work in the market and bring the money home to the family. At that time my mother often told us, "You do not have a father, you have to work. I am a mother and a father now."

What my mother made from her business would be seen only as a little money here in Canada, but in Africa it was enough. She took that money and put it in the bank in Rwanda. We lived comfortably. But in 1994, the government was overthrown and war and genocide came. The government closed the banks and we had to escape the country without the money. There was rebellion all over Rwanda, except in the capital city Kigali where we were. My uncle came for us and took us five children to Cyangugu province in western Rwanda, close to the Congo border and the city of Bukavu. Children could travel without papers, but adults needed documents to travel freely in Rwanda. There were many checkpoints. My mom did not have Rwandan documents since she was not born there so she and Musa stayed behind so he could get forged documents for her. By then Musa had entered the Rwandan army. He had someone in the military drive our mother to Cyangugu to care for us kids. Musa had planned to follow along, but he died in the war.

From Cyangugu we travelled over the border into Congo. We went to Bukavu only a few miles away where there was a United Nations High Commissioner for Refugees (UNHCR) office. We received our refugee status there. They transported us to a refugee camp close by in Sange, close to the border, between Bakuva and Uvira. My mom had a nervous breakdown there, from all the problems and stress – losing everything, no house, no husband, no money, and Musa's death. She left us and went to Uvira, a city a hundred or so miles away, where she had family. My sister Mariamu was very smart. My mother had talked in the past about buying clothes in the market and about her family there in Uvira. Mariamu thought she knew how to find mama, so she got a ride to Uvira from the people who transported the food to the refugee camp each week. Mariamu found our mom easily.

Our uncle returned to the refugee camp and brought us children back to live with my mother and her family. But by 1995, when I was ten, there was war in Congo, very close to Uvira. During an attack, all of us ran in different directions and I became separated from my family. People were dying everywhere. I used my imagination to tell myself that people lying everywhere were sleeping, but they were really dead. I was alone and unsure what to do. I managed to hitch a ride from outside Uvira to Fizi, another city farther south, about one hundred kilometres away. There were government army guys driving a jeep and they let me climb on the back. I held on to the outside spare tire while my feet were on the trailer hitch. It was a very long and very bumpy ride. My middle finger still hurts today from gripping so hard for so long.

In Fizi, all the soldiers were attacked and killed. I lived because I ran to play with the local children, so I looked like one of them. I continued further south on foot to a town somewhere around Makungu. I don't remember the name. There I met a man and his wife; they had no children and took me in. I think they wanted me to become their child. I stayed with them for two months, but I ran away. I knew the war was approaching, and these people did not want to leave their home and all their possessions. I wanted to keep moving and continue to where it was peaceful. So I left for Kalemie a port city on Lake Tanganyika. There I found a Roman Catholic

Church and I stayed there with other refugees. While I was there, I found my sister and brother Mariamu and Amani by looking in the market each day. That is a good place to go when you are looking for someone. At some point they will need food and then someone will know them. They had come by boat to Kalemie. We began to live at another refugee camp there together.

While my younger brother Amani and I were at the refugee camp with Mariamu, I met a man who was the chairman of the camp. He knew our mother. He had just come back from Tanzania, and he told us he had seen our mother there in a refugee camp. I said to Amani, "Go find Mariamu and stay with her. Tell her I am going to Tanzania to find our mother." At that time there was no fighting around Kalamie and it was safe to travel, so I went to where the boats were docked, looking for a boat to take me to Kigoma, Tanzania, about one hundred kilometres away. After asking around, I learned that there was a boat leaving at 6:00 p.m. that night. I was really short, so I stood in line next to a woman and

> Once I was safely on the boat, I walked around looking for food. I waited for people to throw down little bits and then I would pick them up and eat.

pretended to be her son. She did not know I was doing this. In war, children learn how to protect themselves. I was not afraid because there were people all around, and I was busy thinking that when I reached Tanzania I would find my mother and all my problems would be finished.

Once I was safely on the boat, I walked around looking for food. I waited for people to throw down little bits and then I would pick them up and eat. We travelled through the night and reached Kigoma, Tanzania in the morning. I did not know the boat was not a refugee boat, so when the boat docked, Tanzanian immigration people were asking to see passports. I did not have one. I heard a man speaking Kirundi, my language of Burundi, so I spoke to him. I told him why I was on the boat and explained that I was here in Tanzania to look for my mom. He said he would protect me. He and his friend had no passports either and were refugees too. He told me to act like I was working on the boat with them. We all stayed on the boat while the passengers got off. We waited for about five hours until the immigration people had left too. If they had caught us we would have gone to jail. We left the boat and went to the UNHCR offices in Kigoma and presented ourselves as refugees.

At the UNHCR offices, I met a woman I knew named Aziza. She was originally a friend of my sister. She told me that my mother had passed through the offices and had asked her to watch for her kids and tell them where she was. Aziza told me to go to Mtabila refugee camp about one hundred kilometres away. She helped me get a ride on a truck that was going there.

When I reached Mtabila, it took me three days to find my mom again. I went to the market to look for her. There were no cell phones back then. Now cell phones make it so much easier for people to find each other. Finally, I thought I saw her, but I had not seen her in two years and she had changed. She looked older, more wrinkled and sad because she had suffered a lot of stress in her life. She was so thin. As I got closer I thought maybe it was her. Once I could see her face clearly I saw her sign – the raised moles on her cheeks – and I knew it was her. She looked over at me and said "It's you." Seeing her, I felt that now, even though I knew she would have very little, I would be

protected. She closed her stall in the market and said "Let us go home." And then she took me to her home, which was a small tent in the camp and gave me food and water.

My oldest sister Feza and my younger sisters Fatuma and Zayinabu were with my mother in Tanzania. When I got separated from my family in Uvira, Fatuma, Zayinabu and my mom managed to stay together and find a ride on a boat to Kigoma. They passed through the UNHCR offices there, and that is when they came across Aziza and asked her to look out for us. Feza had been alone in another Congolese town, Malindi, and, luckily, she too took a boat to Kigoma where she met Aziza at the offices. That's how she knew to go to Mtabila. I explained I had left Amani and Mariamu back in the Congo, but that I had told them to go to Kigoma. I said I would look for them there. My mother said I should go with Feza back to Kigoma and find them, so we could show them where we were.

We found them in a place called "the stadium" at Lake Tanganyika. This is a common place where people go when searching for their lost family members. I learned from Mariamu that she had had an experience of violence. She was young, thirteen or so, travelling with Amani who was a young boy, maybe seven. A Tanzanian man had said he would help her and give them a room when she did not know where to go. He took her to his home and took advantage of her. It was not her choice. But when you are a refugee, you come to know violence. It happens. So we took them back to Mtabila to mama.

My mama said, "We are a complete family again, so you will all start school." Back in 1994 in Rwanda, I had been in the second grade of primary school. Then we moved to the refugee camp in Congo where I began learning French. I was placed in Grade 3, but I did not stay long. So when we were settled in Mtabila I started grade 3 again. In school, we spoke Kirundi (the language of my family and the main language spoken in Burundi) and I learned more French. I completed primary school – Grades 3 to 6 – and then did an exam for high school and went there for another two years. My mother continued her business, and we lived comfortably at the refugee camp.

I had years of watching my mother work for herself, and I wanted to start a business of my own, but not in Tanzania. I did not want to continue living in the refugee camp, so I asked my mother about us applying to go somewhere else – North America, Australia or Sweden – but she said she was afraid to go to those places because many white people lived there. Her generation believed in a story that whites ate other humans. I know it sounds crazy! At that time, wealthy whites ate a lot of tinned food, and Africans thought this was surprising since we usually eat fresh food from the daily markets. Many people believed that the food in the cans was human flesh. My mom did not feel safe living in a mostly white country. Because I was young and obedient, I did not apply to leave, but I wondered what I could do. I asked a lot of people, and they told me about a country in Africa called South Africa. They said it was like America or Europe. So I went to my mom and told her I wanted to go to South Africa. I said I would come back in a few months. We did not know it was 5,000 kilometres and two countries away. The year was 2001. I was fifteen years old.

I started by asking a lot of questions – that is my nature. So I found a guy taking people without passports to neighbouring Mozambique. Mozambique was between Tanzania and South Africa. He was asking for a lot of money, and I did not have enough. I had already had the experience of passing from

Congo to Tanzania without a passport, so I thought I could make it. I decided to go on my own. The first thing I did was find a map of Africa and look up Tanzania, Mozambique and South Africa. I thought, *all right I can do this!* So first I made my way to Kigoma, a city in Tanzania close to the refugee camp, and from there I took a train to Dar es Salaam, the capital of Tanzania. It took about three days. Once in Dar es Salaam I found the bus station. There were buses going everywhere. I chose a bus to Mtwara in south Tanzania, a city on the Indian Ocean and closer to the border of Mozambique. Once I arrived there, I went to a church and asked people there how I could get to the border. They told me which town to go to and what bus to take. I had to figure out how I would cross. There is a river, Ruvuma, that separates Tanzania and Mozambique. I paid a man to take me to the river on his bicycle taxi. There I paid the police 500 Tanzanian Shillings to ignore that I had no passport and 1,000 TS to another man who took me over the river by boat.

When I reached the other side, there was bush everywhere. I found one restaurant and went in. As I went to pay for some food, I realized my money was gone. I had lost about 100,000 TS worth about $100 US. I did not know what to do. I found a man to bicycle me to the town of Palma if I promised to pay him. It took us all day to get there. Everyone was speaking a language I did not know. It was Portuguese because of Mozambique's colonized history. I went to a church and they paid the man who had bicycled me to Palma. I found someone there speaking Swahili so I asked him for help, and he took me to the government immigration offices. I was worried that I would get in trouble, and I had no money, so I lied and told them I was looking for my family in the local refugee camp, Maratane. My objective was still to get to South Africa, but I thought I could get food and money at the refugee camp first. I was driven twelve hours by truck to the camp. Once I got there, I met people from Burundi and stayed with them. Burundi people are kind to each other. I spent six months in that camp. The camp gave me food, kerosene to cook with and money for petrol. I saved the money and eventually went

There I paid the police 500 Tanzanian Shillings to ignore that I had no passport and 1,000 TS to another man who took me over the river by boat.

to the town of Nampula, still in Mozambique. There I got a job selling cigarettes in the streets. I did that for a year. My objective was to make money to continue my plan of going to South Africa.

I asked around about the capital of Mozambique. People told me it was Maputo, about 2,000 kilometres away. I asked, "Do you think there are refugees there? People from Burundi?" People said yes. I went to the bus station to ask how much it cost to get to Maputo. They told me 1,000,000 Mozambique dollars. That was the adult fare, but children age twelve and under were half price. I had exactly 500,000 Mozambique dollars. I was a short guy, so I said I was twelve years old and that I could pay the half fare. I did not even go back to the camp. There was a bus leaving that day so I just kept on going.

When I reached Maputo, I did not know where to go. I was not afraid because there were people all around me. As a refugee, I had had years of just going and going. When you live the life of having nothing and moving around, it became the only life I knew how to live. I was comfortable. I sat at the bus station watching people coming and going, buying and selling, and I thought, *where can I go now?* All around me people were speaking languages I did not know. Night was coming and I was hungry. I was wearing a T-shirt and a sweater and shorts, no shoes – I grew up without shoes. I walked until I found a hairstyle shop. It was evening, but people were there because that is one place where people often hang around and talk. At night, people sometimes sleep outside because it is hot, so I slept outside by the shop. In the morning, I went in and asked for a little water to drink and use to clean my eyes. But they did not understand my language. I was speaking the Portuguese I had learned in Nampula, but the Portuguese in Maputo was different. They kept calling me "Refugado," stranger in Portuguese.

They finally found someone from Burundi. He asked me many questions, including how I got there and where my mother was. After I told him my story, he said, "This country is very dangerous for kids. You should have stayed with your mom. How will you survive?" I listened to him, but I knew from my experiences in life that I could survive. He cooked food for me and introduced me to the Burundian community in Maputo. These people told me that I had to register with the government to have a licence or permit to be in the city. They were worried that I would be caught by the police and put in jail. When I told them I was planning to go to South Africa, they were concerned, and could not understand why I would want to go there. Everyone said it was a big, dangerous country, and I could get lost there. So I spent time in Maputo with the Burundian community. Someone found me a job calling out to customers in the market to convince them to buy food from a certain shop owner. I was good at it because of my experience in the market at a young age helping my mother. They said, "That boy Asu, he knows how to call people over!" I just kept working and saving my money.

I started asking people how to get from Mozambique to South Africa. Because I didn't have a passport, people suggested I take a longer route where there was less security. My destination was Mpumalanga province, about 420 kilometres away. The whole South African border is fenced with three rows of electric fencing. There are people who have dug tunnels under each of the fences and make their livings opening the ends up for people like me to crawl through. I paid a man to let me use his tunnels. The holes were big, but it was very scary because I went at

night. Once in Mpumalanga, I took a train to Johannesburg. It was a new country and a new world. Imagine a bear used to sleeping in the bush, being deposited in the downtown in the daytime – that was me.

South Africa was not like the Africa I knew; it was different from anything I had ever seen. It was high class, clean and fancy – lots of beautiful cars, good houses and white people. I had only ever seen a few white people, probably tourists, but in Johannesburg there were many, many white people. I felt as though I did not belong there. People were speaking English and Zulu. The languages sounded magical to me. Everything seemed like magic. I was so amazed at everything those first hours in Johannesburg that I had to stop and sit just trying to understand it all. At first I was happy to have reached my goal, but then I became scared – what if the police caught me without a passport? I could go to jail. I had only a bag with a few clothes in it with me, and I did not want to look like a visitor. I was afraid that the police would ask where I was from so I threw the bag away and started to walk.

In Maputo, people had told me to look for hairstyle shops when I reached Johannesburg because they are usually run by people from Burundi or Congo. It was getting late. I felt hungry and lost and scared. Finally, I found a hair shop so I went in and started talking Swahili. The people there were from Zimbabwe and spoke Shona. They did not understand me so they directed me to a person who spoke Swahili. I said "Hey, how are you my brother? I am looking for people from Burundi or Congo or Rwanda." He told me that there were a lot of people from Congo and he took me down the street to a group of them. They said their lives were not easy, the city was expensive, and they did not have anywhere to put me. But they introduced me to a man named Tyson who was from Burundi. He said he would take me in. We went to his house and he sent his wife to the market to get food and water to cook something for me. Tyson had a hairstyle shop and he let me work there with him. I started to learn English, beginning with things like 'Hi there,' 'How are you?' 'Stand up,' 'Where are you going?' If I did an errand for the shop, I knew how to ask for the change. Tyson was very good to me.

Finally, I decided I could survive on my own. I took a job selling fruit in the market for a man from Senegal, and I moved into a house with another guy from Burundi. I wanted to go to school in South Africa, but I was alone and there was no one to help me. I had rent and bills to pay. If I didn't work, I couldn't eat and then I would have nowhere to live. So I quickly accepted that I needed to work and had no time to go to school. I saved all my money. When I was paid I did not spend it. My boss gave me money for my own food, but I ate very little – only a few small snacks throughout the day – so that I could save the money. I ate only one meal, at night, once I was finished work. I saved 2,000 SA rand (about $400 CDN). Then I started to think about the money my boss was making. One plate of fruit sold for ten rand, and I was selling about sixty plates a day. He was making about 600 SA rand. There was good profit! I wanted to work on my own, but I did not have enough savings. So I saved until I had 3,500 rand (about $700 CDN), then I told my boss I was tired of my job and wanted to stop. I lied and said I wanted to move somewhere else.

The next day, I went to the market, bought boxes of fruit and called a taxi to take me to a street corner where I sold the fruit. My boss eventually found me and could not understand why I was there selling fruit again. He would have been angry knowing I was working on my own, so I told him I had found another boss who would pay me more. Originally, my objective was to save enough money so I could travel home to my mother. I was really missing her. However, home was far away and I needed a lot of money for transportation. Over time I became more used to living far from my family and I decided to stay on in South Africa.

Once I had about 6,000 rand (about $1,200 CDN), I decided to leave Johannesburg. There was a lot of crime and if people knew you had money, they would kill you for it. I could not use the bank because I was a refugee with no documents so I cut a sleeve from a sweater and stuffed my money in it and strapped it to my waist under my clothing. I did not feel safe in the streets carrying my money around. I moved sixty kilometres away to Pretoria, the capital city of South Africa. Once there, I found people from my country; they were selling candles and cigarettes in the streets. I decided to start my own business selling those items too. They were easier to sell because they were not heavy like fruit. I moved into a house with a Rwandan man named Damasan. He owned a car. Once I had saved 8,000 rand, I gave 1,500 to Damasan to teach me to drive and I got my license. I was nineteen. I said to myself, *I need to buy a car*, so I bought a Mazda 323 with a 1.6 litre engine. It cost 6,000 rand. It was messed up – the engine would stop unexpectedly – but it helped me to get around easier.

I kept thinking about my mom. We had had no communication for five years. I didn't have the use of email or a cell phone then, but I happened to meet a man from Tanzania who told me my mother had gone to Canada. But I did not know Canada; I only knew New York, California, and Florida. He did not know exactly where she was living, but he knew a Burundian man who lived in Canada, so he gave me his phone number. For two weeks I tried to reach him, and then finally one day he picked up the phone. I said "Ahhh. How are you? My name is Asu and I live in South Africa. Where do you live?" When he told me "Canada," I asked, "Where is Canada, in Europe?" "No," he said. "It's a country in North America. I

I kept thinking about my mom. We had had no communication for five years.

live in the Canadian province of Quebec." When I told him that I'd heard my mother, Rehema Maseruko, was somewhere in Canada and asked if he knew about her, he said, "No, this is a big place. I do not know where she is, but I will give you the phone numbers for more Burundian people. Maybe someone will know her."

I started phoning and when one person didn't know about my mom, I would get more phone numbers of people from the Burundian community in Quebec and call them, one after another. I spent a lot of money on phone bills! Then one day, I spoke to a guy in Sherbrook, Quebec, who knew my mother. He told me to call back the next afternoon and he would have her there to speak to me. The next afternoon when I called he said "Ya, Asu, your mother, she is here and you are going to talk to her." And when he put my mother on the phone, she started to cry. I asked my mom, "How can I come there?" This was in 2006.

My mom was able to help me immigrate to Canada. There was an organization in Sherbrook called Neo-Canadiennes that assisted newcomers, and my mom went there and started the process of requesting immigration for me. She had to send papers to me in South Africa, which was a problem because I did not have a mailbox. But I was able to arrange to get a post office box. I went there every day to look for an envelope from my mom. Once it came, the papers were in French or English, so a Congolese friend, Lambert, who spoke French, helped me fill them out. I took the papers to the Canadian embassy where I was interviewed and asked my mother's name and my siblings' names and ages. Once the embassy person confirmed I was Rehema's son, she told me to go to the hospital and get medical tests and a general physical. I was found to be in good health. I also had to provide my criminal record, which was clear. This all took nine months. Then one day the embassy called and said, "Start preparing, you are going to Canada … tomorrow."

My mom cried when I arrived at her apartment. She looked older. She, Mariamu and Amani had travelled from the refugee camp to Quebec after deciding to apply for refugee status. While living in Africa, my mom had spoken to other Africans who had moved to North America. They told her it was good; the people were nice and it was safe.

People even sent photos. Mariamu helped her apply for refugee status. My sister Feza had returned to Burundi where she was married and had a family. My other sisters Fatuma and Zayinabu, each remained in Mtabila camp with their own families. Once I got settled in Sherbrook, I managed to buy a small used car. I had no job, and of course I wanted to work, but when I asked people how I could get a job, they told me to go to a province where English was spoken, that there would be lots of jobs there. So after one year, I drove alone to Salmon Arm, BC, and got a job planting trees, earning fifteen cents for every tree I planted. I stayed three months and made about $8,000.

Back in Quebec, my mother was not doing well; she had been spending a lot of time shut in her apartment sleeping. She was lonely, had no job and only a few friends. She was missing her other children and felt helpless because she had no money to send to them. I wondered what I could do to help her. So I drove from BC to Alberta to look for a job and a new city for us all to live. The cities in Alberta (Calgary and Edmonton) were so big that I worried they would be too expensive for us. I decided to go to a smaller place, Brooks,

Alberta, where I heard that many immigrants were working in a meat processing plant. But once there, I worried that if I lost my job, Brooks was so small that there would not be many other job options. I decided to check out Lethbridge, a city about five times the size of Brooks. When I asked around about jobs there, I was told to try Sunrise Poultry. I went there and they offered me a job right away. I told them about my family back in Quebec. I said that they did not speak English, but asked if they could get jobs too. The manager promised me they would have jobs when they arrived. The people at Sunrise were nice people and very good to me.

I phoned Amani and told him they must come there right away. I said, "Take everything you have and sell it. Go to Canadian Tire and buy a GPS for your Honda Civic. Put the Lethbridge address in, sit down and drive. But before you come, buy one extra gallon of gas and carry it in your car in case you run out of gas." Mariamu did not come. She stayed in Sherbrook. I never understood why. It took Amani and my mother four days to get to Lethbridge. While they drove, I found a cheap apartment to rent, and when they arrived on a Friday I took them to Sunrise immediately and helped them apply for jobs. On Saturday and Sunday, they slept and relaxed and then started their new jobs that Monday morning. But after three months, Amani returned to Sherbrook. He had fallen in love with a French Canadian woman named Anne-Marie and he was missing her. My mom and I stayed there, but I was ready for a better job. I thought I'd like to have a job as a driver for that company, but they said I needed a high school diploma to work with them. At the time I was taking English classes at Lethbridge College in the evening, but I realized there would be more job choices if I got my high school diploma.

I went to a high school in Lethbridge to ask about starting school there, but my English was not good enough to enroll. Then I talked to my friend Gerard in Winnipeg – we had become friends long ago in Mtabila. He told me about a high school there, College Louis Riel, which was for adults who spoke French. He told me I could learn English later after I received my high school diploma in French. The school year was starting the next week, and I needed to get there right away. He also told me life in Winnipeg was affordable, which I thought was good. I told my mother I was leaving for Winnipeg. She was happy with my decision. She said, "Go and finish your schooling. It is important." So I moved here from Lethbridge in September 2008. I graduated from high school on June 15, 2010. My mom moved to Winnipeg in January 2013. She lives with my family and me. I have a one-year-old daughter and she is happy to be with her.

I am always thinking about ideas to make money. I own a cleaning company with seven employees. We clean bars, restaurants and houses. Owning my own business is a way to make money and to survive. I have also bought a few houses and am now a landlord. I have a lot of other ideas too. My friends back in Africa nicknamed me *boss*. Even in Canada, my friends call me *boss* too. A friend says it is because of my "entre- preneurial spirit."

Life has taught me a lot about people. I can look people in the eyes and feel I know everything about them. I have very good

> My friends back in Africa nicknamed me *boss*. Even in Canada, my friends call me *boss* too. A friend says it is because of my "entre- preneurial spirit."

instincts; many times I am right. Some people tell me I can read peoples' minds. Most people here in Canada are good – I would say seventy percent, while thirty percent are bad. I have thought a lot about employment for new immigrants in Canada, and I see a few main problems. Canadians work very fast, while Africans are used to working in Africa where people work more slowly so they can make their job last longer and continue getting experience. If requested to work faster, it can make us feel like slaves. If our Canadian employers speak quickly and we are still learning English, then we can become confused. This can make our employers mad and we become frustrated at not understanding. Then, if we do not have the words to explain how we feel we become angry inside.

When I worked in Lethbridge, I never had someone who did not like me. But in Winnipeg, I've had some poor treatment. When I first came here and wanted to earn some money while I was going to school, some people pretended not to understand me when I asked for a job. Others understood me, but they would turn and see my face and then look away quickly. They spoke to me without looking in my eyes when telling me they had

no work for me. In my heart, I knew that this was just one of those sad experiences of life.

At one roofing company I worked for, if I touched anything they would yell at me and give me the hardest jobs to do. I've had bosses tell me they did not trust me. Usually, I try to make friends when I sense the other workers do not like me. I try to joke with them and make them laugh, and ask them questions about their lives. But, some people are so angry. One time a co-worker swore at me and yelled, "You people come here, you start gangs, you kill people. If I were the government I'd take you and send you back to your country." I just sat quietly. Even though I was mad, I kept that in and tried to get along. That same guy thirty minutes later said, "Asu, can you lend me $2? I want to get a Pepsi." I did not have the money in my pocket, but I had it in my car. I went out to get it, and since I had a Pepsi there, I brought him both the drink and the money. A few minutes later, he laughed and said, "That was a good joke eh?" I asked, "Which joke?" He said, "All that mean stuff." He told me he spoke to me unkindly so I would become mad and work harder and faster. Then he did a fist pump and laughed. If someone does something bad to me once or twice, I can put it out of my mind, but if it's a third time, well … I think about it a lot. Some nights I have come home from work and not been able to sleep. If I work for myself, I can make good money and live more peacefully.

I am telling you about a few bad things, but I am happy here and I have made a lot of Canadian friends. At first, I did not know how to make friends. I think it is easier if you know more about the Canadian culture. For example, many Canadians are more conservative and serious, so if they say hello to someone they meet, many will nod their heads and have a quiet face. Africans are friendlier and louder; and their faces are more active. But I have learned that this different reaction does not mean you are not liked.

When I was a small boy, I would sit with my mother while she was cooking and she would talk to us kids. (In Africa, there is never enough food, so children always gather around before eating so they do not miss the meal. Unlike in North America, where there is so much food, families sometimes do not even eat together.) My mother used to tell us we had to work. She said, "If you do not have money you are nothing in this world. People will look down on you and see you as lower

class. If you don't have money you will not have transportation to safety if there is a war. Where will you go?" So now, if I have money, I do not have stress. If I have money, I also feel good about myself. When I was young, even when I had on an old T-shirt and it did not fit me, if I had money in my pocket I felt good. That's why, ever since I can remember, I have worked so hard.

Asumani says he is very open to different cultures and to change because he has experienced so much in his life. He makes many astute observations about human nature, culture and life experience. About the cause of war, he said, "People with money use the poor for their own profits. I have seen people in Congo struggle and die because of people wanting something (diamonds for example). Rich people never make mistakes; they think that everything they say and do is right. War comes from rich people." About Canadians, Asu said "They must thank God that they were born in this country. It is safe. There is nowhere else like Canada in the world. That's why every morning, when we wake up, we must be proud to be Canadian."

MARKO

When Christmas comes in Maban there is a change.
People do not think about the bad things that have gone on,
but about community and worshipping God.

When I arrived in Winnipeg in 2002 with my wife and baby daughter, we were the first people from Maban to live here. Where is Maban? Maban is the region of the Republic of South Sudan where we come from, the northeast upper Nile state, close to the Ethiopian border. But it is more than just a geographical region, it is my tribe, my people, my culture, my language, and it was my home.

If you ask me what I miss about Maban, first I would say the land, the nature, and the food we eat there, but then I would start to think of my friends and family, and especially the people who started the word of God there. So, finally I would just have to say that I miss the whole of Maban.

One of the people I miss most is my father-in-law. He is a church elder, a strong man – a man of God. Although he does not read and write, I think he has an ability to memorize scripture. This special gift helps him to preach and quote the bible like someone who has studied theology. If I read him something from the bible, he will then preach with it, as if he had read it himself. When he sings, you can hear his voice above the others – it is always recognizable. He and my mother-in-law are both so kind. We had a great church community and many activities: praying together every night, choir practices and Thursday night Maban Christian Youth Fellowship meetings. My church community became my entire life.

The time of the year I think of my African home and culture the most is during Christmas celebrations. Every time Christmas comes in Canada, I think of our celebrations back home. Yes, Christmas is the 25th, but in Maban preparations for the celebrations begin each year in October and last for many days after the 25th, even into early January. My church, the Sudan Interior Church (SIC), has set up in many towns, so people from all the locations come together to celebrate Christmas. This is also the one time each year that new followers can be baptized in the river. It is such a big event that many, many Maban people come, believers and non-believers. Christmas is for everybody; everyone is welcome.

> Every time Christmas comes in Canada, I think of our celebrations back home.

This is how I remember the Christmas celebrations of my childhood...

The service on the 25th starts at around 10:00 am in Boungtown, the biggest town in our region. People do not have vehicles or bicycles, so those of us from other member churches travel by foot through the night of the 24th and early morning of the 25th. We sing and dance and run as we travel. People from each town carry flags with Christmas slogans as they walk. We are very excited because the day we have been waiting for and preparing for has finally arrived. We reach Boungtown ready for the celebrations on Christmas morning. Over 5,000 people gather there, celebrating all day and night, singing, dancing and listening to the word of God. Then on the 26th, we all begin to spread out, walking from town to town wherever one of our churches is present, until there has been celebrating in every part of the Maban region. On the 26th we divide into two groups: 2,000 to 3,000 go to the north region and the other half go to the south, the region I am from. First we visit Yawaji, and then we divide again the next day with half carrying on to Dangaji, the village I lived in. Next will be Liang, Kanyaji, Kaywaji, Yenaji and Chowaji and so on. In the south, we keep going until we reach the Maban region's border with the Nuer people and west until we reach the border with the Dinka people. Those who go north, travel until they meet the border where the Uduk people have their region. We go to celebrate wherever there is a Sudan Interior Church in the region. People carry on until the New Year, although we still call this long celebration Christmas! Some people even travel until January 6 or 7 and then return to their own villages.

As I say, preparations begin back in October. Each Sunday, at each individual church in the region, we hear preaching about the birth of Jesus Christ and begin to practise our Christmas songs. A big part of our celebration on the 25th is singing. Each church community has a turn singing, and we even have competitions for small prizes. Many years ago a pastor got the idea of forming a United Choir, so each church picks two young people – males and females – to come together with the other chosen singers to form a special choir. Singing is a very big part of our church life because we are praising God and sending a message to the people. In the background of the singing, you will hear *lildeen* (the Maban word for ululating), which is a high pitched call made only by the women when they are excited. It is a happy sound, often heard during weddings. It is a cultural thing, not religious. It is meant to encourage the choir and to show the joy we all feel.

The service takes place outside because the weather is always good and there are too many people to fit into one place. We meet in a big open space with tall trees for shade and tall grasses all around us. The pastor opens with a prayer and we sing a few songs together. Then the United Choir starts to sing for us. That is really great. Afterwards the pastor will read the word of God. People stand in the shade and listen and are mostly silent, except for the small children. A table covered with a cloth is our altar. The pastor walks around reading from his Bible. *Hallelujahs* and *amens* are shouted from the crowd as the pastor reads.

In the 1980s, there was only one pastor for about ten SIC organized churches, and he was not even Maban-speaking. Today, there are eight to ten pastors and about forty organized churches across Maban. Even though we have had great difficulties, the word of God is growing. Today, the church is so much bigger that the celebrations on the 25th now begin in Yawaji instead of in Boungtown, and is only for the south district. The north district meets separately. Also, since there are more pastors, they rotate leading the Christmas program, so each year is a little different. After the pastor speaks, each church group takes a turn singing for everyone. First, there is what we call the marching song. Each choir comes in marching slowly and singing. It is not marching like in an army, but a rhythmic, slow shuffling walk and dance. It takes about ten minutes for each choir to march in before they sing a few songs. Drums play as we sing and you can hear whistles blowing in the background and also something called a *sac-saca,* a shaker made of metal which is folded in a rectangle shape with broken glass inside. People shake it to the beat. You can hear laughter and see a lot of smiles. There are even shouts of encouragement as the choirs sing. In the crowds, some people are carrying *buomks.* They are two- or three-foot-long pieces of wood carved into shapes like guns, sickles and tomahawks. They can be used as weapons for fighting, but here they are shaken in a peaceful way while dancing. The pastor in his white collar and navy blue suit sits on a chair in the front, as do the church evangelists (those who have gone to theology school) and the church elders (respected church members who are responsible for the church). Most people stand, and many dance, swaying from side to side, left foot to right foot, bouncing and clapping. Mothers even dance with their babies in their arms.

After all the singing, we take a break and people are baptized in the river. That is another special thing about the 25th. Our church is Protestant and we do not have infant baptism. I was young – around ten – when I accepted Jesus into my life. Although my parents were pagan, most of my brothers and sisters came to accept Jesus Christ. It all started with my eldest brother Phillip. He is seven years older than I am and we come from the same mother. (My father has two wives. My mother is the first with four children and then my second mother has six.) All the Christians leave their family homes and live in a village together called the Christian Place. There the youth are encouraged to attend public school even though it is a one-hour-and-thirty-minute walk. So when I was nine, Phillip took me to live with him there so I could go to school. Back home, school was not a priority, so this was a great opportunity for me. I became a Christian after watching the work he did for the church. He is now a senior pastor and the principal of Gideon Theological College in Melut, Sudan. They produce a lot of pastors there. I am very proud of Phillip. He has many talents, and he is a gift to the Maban people.

When you accept Jesus into your life you announce it to everyone at church. After that, you take classes and the church trains you. There is a test, and if you pass, you will be baptized at Christmas. If you don't pass, you are trained for another year. The year I was baptized, there were fifty-two of us at the river. They submerged me under the water because this is the way Jesus was baptized. After I was baptized, I felt that I was no longer the same person, that I had started a new way of living.

All those who have been baptized, as well as those who were baptized in the past, take Holy Communion together. We eat very small pieces of bread and drink a red juice that we make from the flowers of the Hibiscus plant. We add the crushed flowers to colour the water red, and add a little sugar. Everyone brings their own glasses, small ones. We do not have a meal on the 25th because there is no budget for that. Instead, we all bring our own snacks. But on the 26th when the south district celebrates together in Yawaji, we have a meal at around 3:00 p.m. We will have made a local stew with pork or lamb or goat meat and we eat it with bread. We do not have snacks or sweets. There is also time for fun activities: soccer, races and drama presentations.

We even have overnight prayers and singing. You might wonder when we sleep. People may go off and have a nap under a tree, but we usually sleep only two or three hours a night. People are so happy and excited that we do not get tired. Also singing helps. We have a kind of friendly competition with singing and this competition makes us stronger. It is a good feeling to do our best, for God and for our church too. Christmas is a time for celebrating.

There is no gift giving as there is here in Canada. Sometimes there are small prizes for the children during the activities. The group I was in won for singing back in the early '80s in Yawaji. We were a group of six kids, and when we won, the prize was six pennies. We took the money to a restaurant and bought a plate of food to share. That is a most happy memory.

In 1983, the civil war between north and south Sudan began again. On December 27, 1984, the southern rebels raided the town of Boungtown where the Christmas celebrations began, and there was a battle. I was in Dangaji, which is a one-and-a-half-hours walk away. The rebels came there too. First they slaughtered our cattle for food, and then the violence escalated. There was fear of women being raped and lack of safety for the community. They left the town after a week, but the peace we had known was gone.

The last time I celebrated Christmas in Maban was 1985. At the time, I did not know it would be my last one. But three months later in early 1986, the violence and living conditions became even worse. Our community was caught in the fighting between the rebels and the Sudanese army. We were afraid of both sides. The rebels were occupying our villages, and if the army thought we were supporting the rebels they would kill us too. About half the people, many children, fled to Ethiopia. This is where the term *Lost Boys and Girls of Sudan* comes from. The other half fled north to Khartoum the capital city of Sudan. We were all looking for a better life with opportunity and education. I was fourteen years old and so my father sent me to Khartoum. There I got a job as a servant in an Arab's home. I worked from five a.m. to six p.m. everyday cleaning. In the evening, I was allowed to go to school for two hours. I slept outside their home in their yard on a mat. I was not a slave because I took the job by my own choice, but I was not treated as a free employee either. I worked there for five years until 1991 when one night I quietly escaped. They never came looking for me and so I got a job as a messenger and cleaner in an office. I made a few trips back home, but never at Christmas.

I met my wife Elizabeth in the Maban community when we were children. We spent a lot of time together at church and her family knew me very well. We always had special feelings for each other. Elizabeth came to Khartoum with her older brother one week after I did in 1986. We were married in 1996. Her parents gave their blessing because they knew me well, and my uncles raised the money for her dowry. It was wonderful to marry the woman I had loved from the time I was a little boy.

The rebels were occupying our villages, and if the army thought we were supporting the rebels they would kill us too.

Khartoum was safe if you stayed out of politics; otherwise you became a target. In April 2000, I finally finished my Sudanese School Certificate (the equivalent of a high school diploma in Canada). To receive my certificate I was required by law to do national service entering the government's army. I would take a three-month army training course and then go to the front line for one year fighting against the rebels of south Sudan. I refused to go for two reasons: my wife was pregnant with our first child and I was not going to kill my brothers in the South. So we escaped Sudan by taking a train from Khartoum north to a city called Halfa. From there, we took a boat on the Nile River to Egypt. After receiving protection from the United Nations High Commissioner for Refugees (UNHCR), we eventually came to Winnipeg.

When Christmas comes in Maban there is a change. People do not think about the bad things that have gone on, but about community and worshipping God. Everyone enjoys Christmas together whether they are Christian or not. It is a time of great joy. Even our Maban elders, people who were there before the missionaries brought the word of God to Maban, come to the church for Christmas.

When I go back to those days in my mind, sometimes I start to cry. My brother sent me a DVD of a recent Christmas celebration back home, and I often watch it. I am thankful to live in Canada now, but I am homesick for a true Maban Christmas. Each Christmas back home made everything feel new in my life. I forgot about what was happening in my regular life. It made my soul feel very rich.

Marko is the only Maban-speaking translator in Winnipeg, because the language is not commonly spoken. When a Maban woman who spoke no English moved to Winnipeg, he quit a good job he liked and was proud of (he had five years seniority and perfect attendance) to translate full time for this woman and her family. Marko was the only link she had to the English language world she had come to. He said that although he had not met this woman prior to her living in Winnipeg, he thought of her as his sister because they were from the same tribe. He felt the only appropriate choice was to help her to the best of his abilities, even if that meant a considerable financial compromise to himself and his family.

ZARA

My mom said it was ten times harder to wait once she had seen my face and knew I would be hers.

*A*lthough Zara is too young to be interviewed, her mother generously shared her story. Zara's account serves to highlight what could be for the estimated forty-two million orphaned children in sub-Saharan Africa. What follows is how Zara might tell her story to someone, perhaps one of her grade school teachers, once she is a little older...

I was born on July 7, 2008 in a little town called Wonji in Ethiopia, Africa. Wonji is a poor town. It has no paved roads, just lots of dust and dirt. People live in little shacks made of metal. None of the kids have shoes and most of their clothes are old and torn. The kids play on a mud hill because there is no grass and no playgrounds like there are here in Canada. But the kids look happy anyway; they always have smiles on their faces. On the day I was born, someone found me alone along the side of the road and brought me to the town's Holy Saviour Orphanage. That's all we know. The people at the orphanage could tell I had just been born because I was not properly cleaned like I would have been in a hospital. No one knows who gave birth to me. People at the orphanage say it is often a young teenage girl from a religious family who is alone, poor and scared will abandon her baby. Usually the family and friends are embarrassed because she is pregnant and ignore her. We'll never know. I hope she is happy now just like me.

That orphanage was a sad place, very poor and run-down. There were mud floors and peeling green paint on the walls. Each metal crib had three or four babies in it, and there were lots of older kids around, ages two to eleven. It was dirty everywhere, not unclean, but dusty like it is outside. There was an old sign on the wall that said *Thank You For Adopting Us. God Bless You.*

My mom says I stayed there only one night. The next day, the orphanage phoned a place called CAFAC (The Canadian Advocates for Adoption of Children). This is an international adoption agency from Manitoba that has a nice foster agency home two hours away in Addis Ababa, the capital of Ethiopia.

That's where I lived for the next eight and a half months until the day my Canadian mom came to get me. My mom wanted to adopt a second child, but things had changed in China where my older sister Lucy is from and adopting someone from there wasn't possible, so my mom decided to apply to Ethiopia. She had to fill out a lot of papers, and it took a long time. Good thing my mom is so organized. People came to her house to see that she was a good mom, and the police had to write a letter saying she wasn't a criminal. It took her fourteen months just to get accepted by CAFAC.

Once I arrived at the agency home, Haregowian, the Ethiopian woman who runs the foster agency, took a picture of me. She prayed over it and asked for help in finding a good match in a mother for me. It was very important to her to pray hard, and to make a good match – which she did! My mom and I both love music, and my mom cannot believe how much alike my auntie Ainsley (her sister) and I are. We both enjoy the same foods and love being with people, and we even have similar expressions on our faces sometimes. Haregowian sure did a good job.

> That orphanage was a sad place, very poor and run-down. There were mud floors and peeling green paint on the walls.

On August 3, 2008, my mom got a phone call at work telling her that my picture was being emailed to her computer at home. She was playing flute in an orchestra performance that night so she had to wait until 11:00 p.m. to go home and see it. She said it was so hard to wait all day. Then she had to send the papers to court in Ethiopia so they could approve her as my adoptive mother. Court closes in Addis Ababa from August to October because it rains so much then, so we had to wait some more months. My mom said it was ten times harder to wait once she had seen my face and knew I would be hers. She knew she was meant to be my mom and she loved me before she even met me! She said she wanted to see my smile right away. In January, my mom got the phone call that she could come and get me. She was told that her name would be on my birth certificate as my parent. She says we're lucky the adoption went through so easily. (That was probably because no one knew anything about my Ethiopian family.)

So Lucy, my grandma who I call Nan and my mom flew on an airplane to get me. They came to meet me on March 26, 2009. I was eight months old. My caregiver at the foster house had to wake me up from my nap, and I was kind of sleepy and not feeling like my usual self. The first visit was a short one, just so we could get to know each other. The next day, they came back and I was much happier. I was wearing the new white dress they had picked out for me. When I was in my mom's arms, I was relaxed. I could tell my mom was happy and relaxed too. I felt very comfortable in her arms because I like people and I am trusting. I also like to be the centre of attention, and they had cookies and toys for me, so I was happy to go with them. But my caregiver cried so much when it was time for me to leave. That was sad. Even though I was not her baby, she loved me and took good care of me and had a hard time saying goodbye. Tears ran down her face and she kept kissing my hand.

The first thing we did was go back to my mom's guest room in a dormitory for the new parents. We sat on the floor there and played. I felt so happy. I especially liked the toys that made sounds. During the first few nights, though, I would wake up and look scared and confused. My mom said that she would talk to me and give me a soother and then I would be comforted and fall back asleep. My mom knew she was lucky, because she could hear the family in the next guest room. Their baby cried and cried all night.

A few days later, we took a very long plane ride home to Canada. So many people came to the airport to meet me. There was my papa and my aunts and uncles and cousins. And my Nan's Ethiopian friends came too. Everyone was tired except me. We went home and went right to bed. I slept so well that first night in Canada.

My full name is Leila Jahzara. Leila means "night beauty" in Arabic and Jahzara, is Ethiopian for "blessed princess." But we just call me Zara. Mom says that I am a party girl. Right from the beginning, I loved people. I like it when they notice me and I can make them laugh. I also really like being with my sister, Lucy, especially when she takes me to the playroom on the third floor of our house and we play toys together. And, of course, I love music. Mom tells me that I sing very nicely – perfectly on pitch. This is uncommon for a girl as young as I am. My favourite song when I was little was *Twinkle Twinkle*. I sang to myself in bed every night in Winnipeg to help me fall asleep. I also liked to dance and clap when my mom played songs for me on the piano. I know she will teach me to play the piano one day. I'll enjoy that because I love to be doing things. The only things that make me grumpy are if we are out somewhere and my mom says we have to go home, or if we spend the whole day at home without an outing. When I am older my mom says she hopes to take Lucy and me on an adventure one day – a trip to China and Ethiopia to explore our pasts.

Where would I be now if it wasn't for my mom and Lucy coming for me? I don't know. I might have stayed in the Wonji orphanage, but I hope not. Maybe I would have lived a life like the kids in the after-school program we visited before they brought me back to Canada. It's a place where kids hang out after school if they have nowhere to go. They learn English, have bowls of oatmeal and play together. My mom showed me a picture she took of a poster that was there on the wall. It showed who the boys and girls from the program were living with. There were forty-eight kids in the program. They were in Grades 1

> My full name is Leila Jahzara. Leila means "night beauty" in Arabic and Jahzara, is Ethiopian for "blessed princess."

to 4. Most lived with their moms or their aunties, twelve lived with their grandparents, five lived with their neighbours and two lived all by themselves. *Child-headed family,* the poster said. I feel sad for those kids. No wonder they like the after-school program so much. A kind man named Bisret runs the program. He told my mom that the only way to break the cycle of poverty is through education. Giving money won't do it, he says. He is very determined to teach the children, and they want to learn. My mom remembers that the children in this program were so welcoming, friendly and polite to her when we visited there. After two or three hours in the program they go to their small homes, which are really metal huts. They eat outside and sleep inside. Mom told me that the money for the program comes from a group in Canada called CHOIR (Canadian Humanitarian Organization for International Relief). She said that CHOIR started when another family who had adopted a baby from Ethiopia wanted to do something kind for other children from their child's village.

My mom doesn't like it when people say I am lucky to be here in Canada. She says I saved her as much as she saved me. She says we were meant to become a family. She says she feels lucky too.

I would like Laura, Zara's mother, to have the last words of this story.

"I think anytime a child comes into the world it is a miracle, whether it is a biological miracle or the different kind of miracle that happens when the stars align and a number of factors come together to bring into your home a child who seems destined to be part of your family. When I sat at my computer and googled "international adoptions" it was just one of a series of fate-filled moments that would bring us to each other. Now I have two children from two ends of the world, each with her own individual story, and we have come together in Canada. I am Caucasian, Lucy is Chinese and Zara is Ethiopian. We are a rainbow family, something that will, I believe, make our story that much more interesting. Our family fits together perfectly. Sometimes I have to remind myself I didn't give birth to my two beautiful children."

RAYMOND

*The Rainbow Community Garden is a multicultural group
with about 112 families from twenty-four nationalities.
I would say we are the world in miniature.*

I was born in Chad in 1978 during a time of civil war and spent more than twenty years surrounded by off-and-on conflict. These conflicts were essentially populations from the North (Muslims) and South (Christians) fighting over the control of enormous amounts of Chadian underground resources – oil, gold, uranium, and iron.

This was encouraged and supported by international oil companies through some western countries. Officially, the North and South were fighting over power; however in reality, the western countries were using the Chadian populations to fight over control of these resources. There were thousands of people killed on both sides and hundreds of thousands of Chadians escaped to other countries. In the 1980s, the first refugee camps in Central Africa were opened in Cameroon and Central African Republic to accommodate those Chadian refugees, many of whom have not returned to Chad until recently.

We were originally a family of four boys and three girls, but then we lost our father, two sisters and one brother in the conflict. My family and our community members had to flee our village several times and stay in the bush sometimes for a few weeks and other times for many months. People were being killed in the village and houses were being burned down by government forces who accused my people of supporting rebel groups from the south (from our native region where the valuable oil sites are). When we were safe enough to return to our village, there was still a serious lack of food and schooling was a difficult situation. We were spending our days out in the bush hunting small animals and collecting wild fruit to eat rather than going starved to school. Because of the hunger, the classrooms were empty. How could we continue to live there?

Then UNICEF came to our town of Koumra and changed everything. They came to assist children and bring foods such as nutritional biscuits, corn beef, and wheat. UNICEF staff began cooking soup and porridge to serve with milk to the students at school, since the famine was huge. In fact, this assurance of food brought us children back to the classrooms. They also helped the town get clean water and gave us medicine and vaccinations. There was a drought and animals were dying in the thousands. The mortality rate in children was very high because of measles, meningitis, malnutrition and other diseases, including malaria. I have the image in my mind of the UNICEF tents in my village, providing us children with porridge and cookies to eat, and with supplies for school.

Then, when I was nine, my father was shot in the head in front of me by men in military uniforms. We do not know who shot him or why since there was never an investigation. Seeing that horror psychologically traumatized me. My mother supported me and helped me to learn to live with the death of my father. Thousands of other Chadian parents and youth were killed in the same

> My family and our community members had to flee our village several times and stay in the bush sometimes for a few weeks and other times for many months.

conditions as my father. My mother decided she would not remarry but devote the rest of her life to our care and education. She remains a widow today.

I went on to complete high school and then to study agronomics, the science of plants. Schooling in Chad is free until the end of high school. In university, students receive government bursaries so it is also free; however, they lose this privilege if they fail their school year. The decision to study agronomics seemed like a natural choice seeing my family once had a farm and, from an early age, I had enjoyed harvesting and eating the fresh produce. In my early twenties, as the war continued, I was forced to flee Chad alone and found myself in a refugee camp in neighbouring Cameroon. My mother and siblings ran in another direction and eventually fled to the Central African Republic where they stayed for a number of months. They returned to Chad once things settled down, but as we were separated I did not know this for some time.

Conditions in the camp made life very tough, so I thought about what I could do to help address the problems. I decided to use my agricultural background to help the refugees initiate some projects. I was already growing vegetables to eat and sell, raising a little money for myself. I had the idea to start a garden with the women, single mothers, and orphans. We grew corn and some vegetables. Everyone had a spot. The United Nations High Commissioner for Refugees (UNHCR) came to visit the project and were impressed with our efforts. They gave us money for tools and fertilizer. In 2000, at the same time I was helping my fellow refugees, I applied for and was accepted to a National School in Ebolowa (the provincial capital city of South Cameroon) that trained people in co-operative management and local development. It was a two-year diploma program for students with an agriculture background.

The refugee camps had very difficult living conditions and I wanted to do something to change that. After I completed my studies I returned to Yaounde, the capital of Cameroon, where refugees were supported by UNHCR. Once I arrived, I introduced myself to the UNHCR, and after interviewing me, they granted me official refugee status. The UNHCR was unable to help us with the costs of living or food, but they provided health care and some scholarships for schooling. As a

they earned, they could send their children to school. I felt extremely proud. The projects were so successful that the UNHCR and Red Cross National Cameroon made a film based on our refugee initiatives. Around the time the film was completed, I was selected to immigrate to North America. I was chosen because of all the projects I had initiated.

Years later, I have had the joy of reconnecting with Henriette Mukesa who I had known in Cameroon and who came to Winnipeg in 2010. A former nurse from Congo and single mother of three, she had participated in my Refugee Integration Project. Henriette has been very committed to the program. I learned that after I left, she took over my work and started training her refugee peers in painting and handicrafts. Her group became one of the UNHCR's official commercial partners taking orders from their office in Cameroon and producing hats, T-shirts, banners etc. with the UNHCR logo. They also produced more items that refugee children sold at local markets in Cameroon, and used the money they earned to buy food and school supplies.

When I was selected to immigrate to North America, I had the choice of going to

group, we continued to work on our gardens, travelling to the rural farm areas for three or four days at a time and then returning to the city. The majority of refugees were illiterate and did not attend school or have any professional skills. Again, I organized different small activities to help them generate funds. For example, women would buy eggs for 20 XAF (Cameroon funds), bake cakes with them and sell them for 50 XAF. I also approached different groups asking them to train these people in painting and handicrafts. The women became self-sufficient. With the money either the United States or Canada. I preferred Canada because of its peaceful reputation. It is seen as the most peaceful country in the world, with many opportunities and human rights. Immigrants in Canada have the same rights as citizens, except they do not have the right to vote. They have the support of the government and the ability to apply for student loans. You cannot find anywhere else in the world like Canada. Back in Africa, Canada is talked about like a heaven, where people can have everything they want without any effort. Canada is a wonderful place, but of course it is not "heaven." After two months here, my friends back in Africa began to contact me asking for money – $300, $1,000, $1,500. I told them I had to work for my money, and that I was not working yet. They became upset – how could I have no money in Canada? I understood their attitude but had to explain that there was a difference between what we know overseas and what it is like living here. Life here was harder than I had imagined.

English was difficult to learn. When I arrived here, I spoke no English. I did speak French, but that language was not as prevalent in Canada as I had hoped. I realized I must go to school. It was hard work, but with the help of different programs and my determination, I learned enough to attend Red River College's Language Training Centre. Once my English was stronger, I took the Community Development /Community Economic Development (CD/CED) Program at Red River College. After graduating from it, I started working for Community Education Development Association (CEDA) in November 2009 as a community development co-ordinator at Hugh John Macdonald School where I continue to work today. I am also currently taking courses at the University of Winnipeg to complete a degree in Urban and Inner City Studies.

In 2008, as a student from RRC in the CD/CED program, I did a practicum placement at Knox United Church with the people of the Central Park Community. I found myself in a similar situation to the one I had been in at the refugee camp, because the community needed help to grow food. I had direct experience in this. I felt happy and useful in sharing my knowledge with these people. Newcomers have a real challenge adjusting to Canadian food. They cannot find the leaves and vegetables they want, and if they do, they are costly and often the flavour is poor. As a solution, newcomers may eat junk food, which has an impact on their health. Missing the foods of their home countries makes many people feel lonely and homesick. Immigrants in the community told me that the problem of food adjustment was having a real impact on their integration, so I had the idea of starting an organic, tropical community garden. The University of Manitoba donated the land. The community members, especially the women, were very excited.

In June 2008, we began the project with six families. How to find seeds was a concern, but fortunately I had brought some tropical seeds with me from Cameroon. We planted many leaves: sorrel, sweet potato leaves, exotic spinach, amaranth and okra. We also grew vegetables native to Africa – cucumber and squash – as well as variety of Canadian vegetables. The flavours were delicious, and we felt the project was a success. I felt satisfied with that; however, I wanted to do more to help because I knew the needs were huge. Now in 2012, our gardening community, which is called the Rainbow Community Garden, is a multicultural group with about 112 families from twenty-four nationalities. I would say we are the world in miniature.

We have more than plant growth; we also have people growth. The children are happy to eat the dishes of their home country and became interested in the garden too. Parents and children are working together just like they used to in their home countries. In the African way, gardening means community and sharing. Community members come together to help each other. It is good for the kids to be there instead of hanging around downtown where gangs can target them and bad things can happen. The garden gives individuals from different cultural backgrounds the opportunity to interact and become closer than they would if they had met downtown. Because most gardeners don't understand each other's languages, the only way to communicate is to practice their English. The garden site has become a place for talking and compassionate listening as former refugees share stories and cry

> In June 2008, we began the project with six families. How to find seeds was a concern, but fortunately I had brought some tropical seeds with me from Cameroon.

together. They also talk about such things as weddings, traditions, and recipes. A feeling of community has formed, and this has helped many with their loneliness and homesickness. Not only do they grow foods for their own families and save money, but they also sell the leftovers at the market in Central Park in the summer months and make some extra money. Close by, the Faculty of Agriculture has garden space and we have all gotten to know the plant science students. They were happy to meet the newcomers. We showed them the food we were growing, and they were especially interested in our wild amaranth. It is known in Canada as pigweed and was eaten by early Canadian settlers. Our variety was new to them, so we all found our interactions very interesting. Many good things have come from our Rainbow Community Garden.

I want to promote good things happening in our community too. I feel I am doing that with my current job in community development. I want to help create a safer, more self-reliant downtown community. That's why I am striving to help others around me, especially the immigrants and newcomers with poor literacy, who cannot get ahead in the Manitoba labour market. Many newcomers

had never attended school or an English class before arriving here. It can take one to two years of daily schooling just to learn the basics. During that time, newcomers can experience culture shock and start to lose hope. The newcomer youth are approached by gangs very early, and that can get them into trouble. I feel good about my work with the community.

In 2008, with help from the Canadian government, my son Israel came from Chad to join me in Canada. Israel had been living first with his mother and then with my mother after his mother got engaged. He was happy to meet me after only seeing me in photos my family had shown him. Israel's mother had escaped from Chad when I fled to Cameroon. At that time, I did not know that she was just two-weeks pregnant. In fact, I only heard the news of Israel's birth after living for three years in Cameroon. When he came to Canada, he could not say one English word so I placed him in full-day French school. Today at age twelve, he is doing very well in school and loves soccer and art. Now his oral English is better than mine!

Today, my mother and sisters are living in Chad. I would like to bring them to Canada but I do not have the financial resources to meet the government requirements because

I share my income with them every month. I feel it is my duty to help my mother in her old age since she decided not to marry another man after my father was killed and devoted herself completely to her children.

As soon as I got settled in Winnipeg, I went looking for the UNICEF offices. I had volunteered for the organization in Africa, and I wanted to help them again. In my mind, I carry a moral debt to UNICEF for all they gave to me in my early years. I do not think I would have completed my schooling and become the person I am today without all the support UNICEF has given me. The staff is wonderful. By volunteering with them, I am paying back this debt and freeing myself. It is a way for me to give to others what I received from UNICEF during the civil war.

Here in Winnipeg, I have found what I was expecting – peace, rights for everybody and freedom. If you have the motivation, nothing can prevent you from succeeding here. I want to be a product of Canada's graciousness. Thanks to this country, I am here and getting opportunities. I really feel a sense of belonging and Winnipeggers are amazing souls! I have received a lot of support, and I keep thinking *how can I help others?*

Raymond tells a fascinating story about his year of birth. He was born in 1978, but his birth certificate reads 1973. Chadian students lost years of school due to the civil wars and in the 1980s priority for Grade 1 was given to children who were ten years of age or older. Raymond's late father, who was then still alive, was very passionate about having his children educated so he had a friend change Raymond's birth certificate to read 1973 so he would be allowed to enter school sooner. Raymond says he was the smallest child throughout his entire school years and this earned him the nickname Moustique, *the French word for mosquito.*

In 2009, Raymond was honoured twice for his work with the community. First UNICEF *Canada gave him their National Award in Community Service on behalf of its Prairie Region, and he also received the Manitoba Food Matters Provincial Golden Carrot Award in the community food champion category.*

Epilogue

I believe in the power of personal stories. Sharing our stories can transform us. We all need to be heard and to know that we matter. Stories feed our souls' desire to connect with each other. As the author Isak Dinesen said, "to be a person is to have a story to tell." One of the objectives of this book is to honour the stories of African Canadians. By listening to these stories of courage and resiliency, we, as witnesses, can grow too. I know I have.

Think of it – coming to a country you have never visited and likely know nothing about; coming to cold and snow, an unfamiliar culture, probably a new language, overwhelming employment challenges and major life-altering compromises. And you've been forced to leave behind the comfort (though imperfect) of what you've known and has been a part of you forever – friends, family, homeland – all because of the personal suffering brought on by conflict and violence you have had no control over.

How does it feel to have to start anew?

Like a baby being born again, is the answer given by Muuxi, one of the contributors in this book. He and all those who tell their personal stories in these pages have learned, as Eleanor Roosevelt terms it, "to take the next thing that comes along" optimistically and courageously. That is resiliency. These people remind us that the human spirit burns brighter than the horrors that threaten to extinguish it. It is that steadfast and generous spirit that causes many of the contributors to call themselves "lucky;" some prefer the word "blessed." Both feelings are rooted in gratitude and speak to the strength and hope of these individuals, and beyond them of the communities they represent. Equally, Canada is lucky to have these individuals as part of our country. Their resilience, determination and spirit strengthen and enhance our country.

We Canadians have reason to feel great pride in our country, which for many years has been a world leader in welcoming immigrants. Another point of pride is that Manitoba sponsors one of the highest provincial per capita numbers of immigrants in Canada. To me, that means Manitoba is a world leader in welcoming and assisting immigrants. My hope is that all levels of governments in Canada will enable these provincial and national trends to continue. In sharing the bounty of our country, our understanding and compassion is expanded, and our lives are enriched.

But what about the suffering that still happens right here to those very people we promise safety and peace? One particular story that could not be included in this book haunts me and it illustrates the need for further awareness. This is a story about a woman I'll call Z. A few days after Z gave her interview for this book, she had a post-traumatic stress disorder crisis from retelling her story. This resulted in her being admitted to the psychiatric ward of a hospital for medical assistance and in her children being temporarily removed from her home. Her story is another one that illustrates the resiliency that immigrant life demands in order to heal from prior sufferings. It also points to what we as Canadians need to look at to ensure that we do offer a haven and not further agony for those who come here to start over.

During our conversation it was clear that Z is grateful to be in Canada. She was amazed by something as simple as the abundance of food here and how easily available it is, because as a little girl she knew the desperation of extreme hunger: eating only tree bark and algae for weeks on end while on the run from violence. But Z was candid about her experiences of racism in Winnipeg coming from fellow students in the classroom and even strangers on the street. She spoke about a time when she was visibly pregnant and pushing her young child down the street in a stroller. A woman stopped her and said,

"What are you doing here? You people just keep having babies. It's not your country. Go back to your own damn country!" Z said that at times like that she has wondered if it would be better to die back in Africa than to have people talk to her this way in her new country. She wonders how she is going to raise her children to be good in a country where they could be subjected to this kind of treatment. She said, "I need people to understand; God created us to be all colours. But God also created us to love each other – black, white, whatever colour. We have the same blood, the same heart, two eyes; everything is the same except our colour. I need people to hear that. Being quiet hurts. We need to talk."

My hope is that this book brings about the conversations and the understanding that Z is hoping for. Most of us have not experienced the violence that brought most of the book's contributors here to Canada, but if we can see some part of ourselves in their stories, we can feel a connection. This better enables us to welcome our newcomer friends, offer them a safe place to begin again and also to have our own lives enriched in the giving.

Acknowledgements

To the eighteen people who fearlessly and optimistically agreed to share their stories for this book; everything began with you. Your stories and trust have taught me about the human spirit. You are each very fine individuals and Canada is lucky to have you; so is this book. I give you my deepest gratitude.

To Keith Levit, whose photography illuminates and enhances the pages and cover of this book. This book is so fortunate to have you. Thank you for your generosity of spirit, artistry, patience and sincere love of people. Your work captured each subject perfectly, helping to make this book unique. Thank you to Harriet Zimmer who serendipitously suggested Keith to me.

To Lloyd Axworthy, who kindly wrote the foreword lending his name and voice to this book. Thank you for your integrity, character and commitment to affecting positive change.

To those who suggested or introduced me to the participants in this book: Omar Adan, Abdi Ahmed, Mwumvaneza Azarias, Amadou Cisse, Noelle DePape, Julien Fradette and Suzanne Snider, Rob Geisbrecht, Andrea LeBlanc, Laura MacDougall and her mother Judith, Bill Millar, Frances Molaro, and Tricia Schers.

To the places that shared their space for interviews: Gateway Church, Holy Redeemer

Church, Immanuel Fellowship Church, Knox United Church, St. John Brebeuf Church, St. Ignatius Church and Trinity Baptist Church.

To the many people (most whom I was meeting for the first time) who kindly and generously let me ask them questions so that an idea could take shape to become this book. You remind me that there are a lot of good people in the world.

To my many friends who asked about the project and listened, and gave ideas or encouragement, especially Beth McDonald, Pat and Barb Mahon, Jane McDonald, Leslie McLeod, Marjolein Drybrough, Karen Fuhr, Noelle DePape, S. Laurette Doiron, S. Lesley Sacouman, Margaret Proven and my book club of exceptionally smart women. Thank you as well to Joanne Klassen who taught me about the importance of personal story.

To Stephanie Nolen author of *28: Stories of AIDS in Africa*. The excellence of your work and your subjects' lives inspired me. Thank you.

To Catherine Shields, Joe McLellan, Paula Isaak, Jen Moncreiff, Denise Ommanney, Renate Schulz and Paul Mahon who read the early draft and gave honest and helpful feedback.

To the Winnipeg Foundation for valuing these stories and honouring them by funding the distribution of this book to 290 school libraries in Winnipeg.

To all the staff at Great Plains Publications and especially Ingeborg Boyens. Thank you for having faith in me as a rookie. Ingeborg, from you I have learned about honesty, respect and professionalism.

To Marjorie Anderson, my friend and first editor of this book. I am so grateful for you and to you. Thank you for everything you have done to not only make this a better book, but to help it find its way into the world. Your continuous encouragement, generosity and wisdom amaze me.

Finally to my husband Paul, and my children Kendra, Mark and Andrew. Thank you for supporting me, listening to me and loving me. You guys are the best!

AMDG

Some Great Books

Beah, Ishmael, *A Long Way Gone*, Douglas and McIntyre, Vancouver, 2008.

Bul Dau, John, *God Grew Tired of Us*, National Geographic, Washington DC, 2007.

Eggers, Dave, *Out of Exile: Narratives from the Abducted and Displaced People of Sudan,* McSweeney's Books, San Francisco, 2008.

Eggers, Dave, *What is the What?*, Vintage Canada, 2007.

Goodwin, Debi, *Citizens of Nowhere*, Doubleday Canada, 2010.

Ilibagiza, Immaculée, *Left To Tell: discovering God amidst the Rwandan holocaust*, Hay House, Carlsbad California, 2006.

Kidder, Tracy, *Strength in What Remains*, Random House, New York NY, 2010.

Leddy, Mary Jo, *At the Border Called Hope: Where Refugees are Neighbours*, Harper Collins Canada, 1997.

Maskalyk, Dr. James, *Six Months in Sudan: A Young Doctor in a War-Torn Village*, Doubleday Canada, 2007.

Moorehead, Caroline, *Human Cargo: A Journey Among Refugees*, Vintage Books, London, 2006.

Nutt, Dr. Samantha, *Damned Nations: Greed, Guns, Armies and Aid*, Signal, Toronto, 2011.

Pipher, Mary, *The Middle of Everywhere: The World's Refugees Come to our Town*, Harcourt, New York, NY, 2003.

Shannon, Lisa, *A Thousand Sisters*, Seal Press, Berkeley California, 2010.

Zainab Salbi, Zainab, *The Other Side of War: Women's Stories of Survival and Hope*, National Geographic, Washington DC, 2006.

Index

Halfa, Sudan, 191
Hassan, Mahamud, 84, 85
Hawadle, 88
Health Sciences Centre Hospital, Winnipeg, 153
Hema, 51, 160
Heritage Fellowship Church, 152, 153
Holland, Manitoba, 74
Holland, Europe, 96
Holy Saviour Orphanage, 193, 194
Hospitality House, 103
Hugh John MacDonald School, 203
Humankind International, 29
Hunkings, Marion, 150
Hunkings, Willis, 150, 151
Hutu, 32, 135, 168

Iliff School of Theology, Denver, 108
Ilorin, Nigeria, 147, 148
Immanuel Fellowship Church, 152, 153
immigration
    application, 96;
    history of, Manitoba, 104, 155;
    interview for, 73-74, 76, 96, 112-13;
    rights in Canada, 203;
    rural living, 69, 78-79, 115-16;
    skilled worker, 96;
    sponsorship, 74-75, 93, 99-102, 179;
    U.S. government policies, 111, 113
India, 135, 136
integration, 25, 43-44, 116-17, 183, 207;
    childhood 110-11;

choices/fitting in, 59;
    ease of, children, 58, 108;
    expectations, 162;
    first year, 98-99;
    success at, 64
international adoption, 193-97
International Centre, 100, 103, 104
International Federation of Journalists, 42
International Red Cross Network, 160
Immigrant and Refugee Community
    Organization of Manitoba (IRCOM), 58, 116
Ireland, 124, 155
Italy, 114

Jinja, Uganda, 123
Johannesburg, South Africa, 176, 178
Johnson Sirleaf, Ellen, 17
Juba, South Sudan, 124, 1218

Kalemie, DRC, 170, 171
Kampala, Uganda, 54, 55, 56, 122, 124,
Kanyaji, South Sudan, 187
Kaywayji, South Sudan, 187
Kenya, 29, 31, 32, 42, 89, 123, 124, 135-36
Khartoum, Sudan, 121, 190, 191
Kigali, Rwanda, 168, 169
Kigoma, Tanzania, 171, 172, 174
Kiira College, 123,
Kisangani, DRC, 48, 49
Kitchener, Ontario, 147, 148, 150, 151, 152
Kosovo, 99

L–R: Marko, Seid, Sally
Following page: Zara and her sister